A UNIQUE CHILD SERIES

Health and Wellbeing

Growing and developing ■ Physical wellbeing ■ Emotional wellbeing

by Anne O'Connor

Published by Practical Pre-School Books, A Division of MA Education Ltd, St Jude's Church, Dulwich Road, Herne Hill, London, SE24 0PB.

Tel: 020 7738 5454 www.practicalpreschoolbooks.com

© MA Education Ltd 2014

Design: Alison Cutler **fonthill**creative 01722 717043

All images © MA Education Ltd. All photos taken by Lucie Carlier.

ISBN 978-1-909280-70-0

Introduction:
Health and wellbeing

There is a great deal of debate about the nature of wellbeing – how we recognise and foster it in children, how we measure it and how we safeguard it. As early years practitioners we need to be aware of the aspects of health and wellbeing that particularly affect babies and young children and be sensitive to the external factors that can make a difference to individual children, even before they are born.

Our understanding of physical wellbeing needs to include not just healthcare, nutrition and hygiene, but also the importance of movement and activity and the way that physical development underpins all other development in the early years. This includes emotional and social development, which is fundamental to wellbeing and is dependent on consistent loving relationships.

The child's relationship with their parent(s) and family is the first and most important relationship to be promoted. We must therefore focus on the wellbeing of the parent(s) too, as the experiences of children are inextricably tied to the welfare of their parent(s) and families – and *their* resilience to stress and challenge.

Studies into the effects of stress, vitamin and mineral levels, alcohol and other drug use during pregnancy, show us that even before birth the parents' health and general wellbeing has an impact, not just on the wellbeing of the child whilst in the womb, but also their long term health and development.

Nor can we forget that the wellbeing of practitioners also makes a difference to the wellbeing of the children we work with. We carry a huge responsibility for the care and education of babies and young children, while they are with us. Today's youngsters are likely to have experienced care outside the home in several different forms before they reach the milestone of starting school at the relatively young age of four. This has major implications for all children but particularly those from vulnerable families where other factors such as poverty, poor mental and physical health and lack of social networks can collide to make life very challenging. The highest quality support, care and developmentally appropriate education is essential for every child but for vulnerable children and their families it is absolutely crucial if we are to make a difference to the quality of their lives – and to even begin to address what politicians refer to as the 'gap' between the educational achievements of vulnerable children and those of less vulnerable or disadvantaged children.

Yet early years practitioners (including teachers in nursery and reception classes) are often struggling to meet the demands of targets and ever changing policies that compete with our long-held professional responsibility to provide the best possible environment for young children's care and education. This can have a very negative impact on our own wellbeing and on our ability to do the job properly.

We need to be very clear that the health and wellbeing of children, their families and the practitioners who work with them, should not be in competition with each other.

Where the environment and practices support the wellbeing of all, then the provision for children will be better and more successful in its outcomes. This book aims to address these issues by looking at the key areas, exploring the issues and providing a checklist at the end of each section that considers the best possible experiences and outcomes for the child, alongside the experiences and outcomes of the parents and practitioners too.

The sections focus on the three areas of 'Health and Well-being' as described in the Early Years Foundation Stage Themes and Commitments: A Unique Child (2008) with reference, where appropriate, to the statutory requirements for the EYFS (2012).

Throughout the book there are pauses for reflection with 'something to think about' that allows the reader to consider their own experiences both as a child and as an adult, their needs and responsibilities as a professional and some added questions to challenge and provoke further reflection.

Further information, including useful books and websites can be found at the back of the book in the References section.

Section 1: Growing and developing

Right from the start

One of the four guiding principles that shape practice in the early years is that

> 'Every child is a unique child, who is constantly learning and can be resilient, capable, confident and self-assured'. (EYFS framework 2013: 3).

But it is sometimes hard to keep in mind the 'uniqueness' of each child when we are swamped by advice and directives that seem to present a 'one size fits all' approach to child development. Babies are born varying in weight and length and grow up to be adults of different height and body proportions. Our growth is largely determined by factors of heredity, hormones, nutrition and emotional influences (Bruce, Meggit and Grenier 2010) and is easily measured. We use centile charts to plot the height (length), weight and head circumference of babies and children. These can then be used to compare growth patterns of an individual child against the range of growth seen in a large number of children of the same age and gender. These can be helpful in providing reassurance that within a wide range, a child is still developing 'typically'. Outside of this range would suggest that the child is developing 'atypically' and should be monitored more closely. The words typical/atypical are more helpful than normal/abnormal when describing children's growth and development.

Physical development is more complex than growth and is *assessed* rather than *measured*. Some aspects of physical development are very visible, for example the skills and abilities that a child acquires as they gain increasing control of their bodies, but others, such as the development of the senses and inhibition of primitive reflexes are less so. Find out more about Physical Development in Section 2.

Good beginnings

Long before there were statutory requirements for the early years, nursery practitioners were well aware of the importance of children's health and wellbeing. Much of the early work in developing nursery schools was to provide healthy environments for children living in industrialised towns and cities, where they would be provided with healthy food to nourish their bodies and healthy indoor and outdoor activities to nourish their minds. More recently we have become aware of the implications of the health and wellbeing of the parents, particularly the mother, on the subsequent health and wellbeing of their children, so that what happens before the child is born is just as crucial as what happens afterwards. As well as the impact of post-natal depression, research suggests that stress and anxiety during pregnancy may well effect a child's later years and be a predictor for later problems with behaviour at 4 years old. (Underdown 2007).

Pre-term births

In the past, the concerns for a child born prematurely (or 'pre-term') were mostly about their health and medical needs. Now we are increasingly becoming aware of how even a moderately early birth of a month to six weeks can have an impact on a child's general development. This is because a huge amount of growth and brain development takes place in the last weeks inside the womb and an early birth can cut this short. Pre-term births are often stressful, and in the past, babies born early were often exposed to invasive and painful medical procedures, as well as being kept isolated in incubators. Neonatal practice now recognises the importance of warmth and sensitive touch in the development of early attachment and bonding between the child and their family and now tries to reduce the impact of painful procedures on the baby.

As more children survive extreme pre-term births as well as moderate, we need to be well equipped to understand the implications for their health and general development and the behaviours we might see as a result. In particular, we need to be aware that for some children, their birth date could bring their entry into school forward a whole year earlier than their due date would have done. This may mean they have particular needs because of their potentially lower levels of physical and cognitive maturity. However, this may not be the case for all and as you will read many times throughout this book, children are individuals with individual rates of growth and development. It is our personal knowledge of children that enables us to make the best decisions for them based on their individual needs.

Economic factors

Children's health and wellbeing are a complex mix of the genes they inherit (nature) and the environment in which they live (nurture). As we have already considered, this environment is very much affected by the health and wellbeing of the people who care for the child, as well as their experiences, their beliefs and their attitudes.

Often the first thing we think of with regards to a child's environment is the level of poverty or economic deprivation with which they live. Despite government attention and political will, child poverty is still a major concern. Studies such as that by Bradshaw (2003) suggest that rates of low birth weight, infant mortality and child mental health are much higher among poor children, although other health indicators such as asthma are not associated with poverty. (Foley 2008). Being poor does not have to mean a child must be unhealthy. Similarly, being comfortably off does not automatically provide a child with good health and wellbeing. But much as it is important to remember we are dealing first with the child, and secondly with the economic condition of their parents, we also mustn't forget that poverty can make life more challenging for even the most robust families. In recent times, the numbers of children treated for malnutrition in hospitals has risen quite dramatically. Many believe this to be due to economic recession and the impact of austere welfare cuts. (Taylor-Robinson et al. 2013).

Neglect and abuse

Regardless of levels of economic wealth and education, it is a sad fact that quite large numbers of children will experience neglect and abuse. Between 2009 and 2011, The NSPCC, the UK charity dedicated to fight cruelty against children, reported that neglect was a factor in 60 per cent of the 139 serious case reviews (where a child died or was seriously injured). In 2012, a total of 50,573 children were on child protection registers or subject to a child protection plan in the UK and research indicates that abuse and neglect are both under-reported and under-recorded, so the situation is probably even worse than figures suggest.

Statutory Requirements

3.4 Providers must be alert to any issues for concern in the child's life at home or elsewhere. Providers must have and implement a policy, and procedures, to safeguard children. These should be in line with the guidance and procedures of the relevant Local Safeguarding Children Board (LSCB).

3.5 A practitioner must be designated to take lead responsibility for safeguarding children in every setting. Childminders must take the lead responsibility themselves. The lead practitioner is responsible for liaison with local statutory children's services agencies, and with the LSCB.

3.6 Providers must train all staff to understand their safeguarding policy and procedures, and ensure that all staff have up to date knowledge of safeguarding issues.

3.7 Providers must have regard to the Government's statutory guidance 'Working Together to Safeguard Children'. If providers have concerns about children's safety or welfare, they must notify agencies with statutory responsibilities without delay.

Indications of neglect

The statutory requirements outline the signs practitioners should be aware of that may indicate neglect or abuse.

Action for Children, a UK organisation campaigning to support the most vulnerable and neglected children and young people states that:

A child experiences neglect when the adults who look after them are not providing for their needs in an adequate way. This may be in one or more of these aspects of the child's life:

- ○ *basic daily care: food, clothing, shelter and warmth*
- ○ *safety, health care and stability*
- ○ *emotional warmth*
- ○ *stimulation*
- ○ *guidance and boundaries.*

The long term impact that neglect can have on a child's health and wellbeing mustn't be underestimated. Not only distressful to the child while it is happening, neglect can affect their educational development and lead to a wide range of physical and mental health problems in later life. These in turn, can lead to difficulties parenting their own children and so the cycle of neglect by parents is not always intentional – it may have its roots in the parents' own neglectful experiences. Neglect is about the basic needs that are persistently lacking in a child's

life, such as food and warm clothing, but also security, love and emotional warmth. It is a complex issue and Action for Children suggest the following as more specific indicators of possible child neglect:

- frequently going hungry

- frequently having to go to school in dirty clothes

- not being taken to the doctor when ill

- regularly having to look after themselves alone at home under the age of 16

- being abandoned or deserted

- living in dangerous conditions, for example around drugs, alcohol or violence

- finding it difficult to adapt to school

- ·children who are often angry, aggressive or self harming

- children who find it difficult to socialise with other children.

The document 'What To Do If You're Worried A Child Is Being Abused' (https://www.gov.uk/government/uploads/system/uploads/attachment_data/file/190604/DFES-04320-2006-ChildAbuse.pdf) provides detailed advice and guidance about what you should do if you have concerns about a child's welfare.

To feel loved, nurtured and cared for is the right of every child. But when their home circumstances are less than ideal, the warmth and care they receive in early years settings can make a big difference to the quality of their lives. 'Skilled, observant practitioners, who build strong supportive relationships with children and families, are well-placed not just to spot neglect and abuse when it happens, but also to be part of the solution'. (O'Connor 2010).

Family life

Of course, when things go well enough in families, as we hope they do for most children, then wellbeing is more assured. We recognise nowadays that families are organised in many ways and that the 'standard' family of two parents, two children and a dog is no longer considered the only way for a family to thrive and flourish. Blended families, step families, extended families, same gender parents, single parents, adoptive and foster parents are all part of the glorious tapestry of family life in the 21st century, providing children with happy and stable home lives. But all families benefit from a bit of extra support and guidance at some time or other.

Something to think about

○ How do you help children to recognise and appreciate the many ways there are of creating and building a family?

○ How do you balance the needs of very vulnerable families and children with those who appear to be coping?

○ How do you spot a family who might need a little extra help, long before a crisis occurs?

In many areas, local Children's Centres have not only provided the kind of outreach and family support needed by vulnerable families but also offered a much needed centre of expertise for all parents to draw on, for advice and information, as well as opportunities to socialise and play with other parents and children. From the earliest days of the Pre-school Playgroup Association (PPA) now known as the Pre-school Learning Alliance (PLA), children have benefited when their potentially isolated parents have more opportunities to meet and make friendships while their children played. We know that parental wellbeing is a key factor in children's wellbeing so we need to fight to keep universal services available in every neighbourhood. In these uncertain times of global and economic instability, ensuring the wellbeing of future generations depends on how well we look after today's children and their parents.

Prime times

Stages of development

By and large there are some stages of development we expect most children to go through and these milestones can be helpful in monitoring a child's progress and flagging up a concern when progress is not going as we expect. There are several excellent child development books, online resources and even an 'app' providing rough guides as to what to expect at certain ages (see References).

However, child development guides need to be used with a degree of caution. Parents, in particular, need to be reassured that children are individuals with individual rates of growth and development.

'Development Matters', the non statutory guidance for the Early Years Foundation Stage, for example, makes the following statement on each page.

'Children develop at their own rates, and in their own ways. The development statements and their

order should not be taken as necessary steps for individual children. They should not be used as checklists. The age/stage bands overlap because these are not fixed age boundaries but suggest a typical range of development'. (Development Matters 2012).

The more recently published 'Early Years Outcomes' (DfE 2013) is a reduced version of Development Matters, focusing purely on the goals and outcomes from the 'Unique Child' column. Practitioners are encouraged to use these in a 'best-fit' approach to assessing a child's development. However, these are relatively narrow statements that don't always allow for the unique ways in which children make progress and develop.

It is true that a child's development and progress in the early years is at its most rapid, with change being noticeable on a weekly if not daily basis, but sometimes children will take time to consolidate a new skill or stage of development. Reaching or rushing through a stage early is not always best for a child's long term development. Equally important, however, is the fact that there are some critical or sensitive periods when key aspects of development should ideally take place in order to build foundations for later development.

Prime areas of the EYFS

The PRIME AREAS of early learning as outlined in the EYFS (2012) are:

- physical development

- communication and language development

- personal social and emotional development

An important feature of the prime areas is that they are 'time sensitive'. This means that if they are 'not securely in place between 3-5 years of age, they will be more difficult to acquire and their absence may hold the child back in other areas of learning'. (Moylett and Stewart 2012).

Bruce, Meggitt and Grenier (2010) describe how important it is that children should be 'helped appropriately, at their optimal or best times of development, in a stimulating environment, by people who are sensitive and observant of what an individual child can manage (regardless of norms and average ages for doing things)'.

Sharing concerns with parents

Good communication with parents helps to make sure that the best use is made of these optimal times and that the individual child's unique progress is understood and appreciated. Any concerns can then be comfortably shared between parent and practitioner and careful monitoring will ensure that concerns continue to be addressed. Ideally, a good relationship between a child's key people and the parent(s) means that there will already be an atmosphere of trust and familiarity, so that sensitive issues can be explored informally and in a relaxed way, when they meet regularly.

Sometimes, however, you may have to raise concerns with a parent you do not know very well, particularly in the early days of a key person relationship. (See more about the key person approach in Section 3.)

Ask yourself first, how **you** would want to be treated in the same situation. Be aware of the courtesy and consideration you would hope for and be sensitive to the parent's situation. They may already be feeling anxious and insecure and a challenge about their child's development may make them react defensively or even aggressively. Encouraging them to talk about their child, sharing positive strengths and achievements, opens the way for a more comfortable conversation.

- If English is not their first language then find an interpreter wherever possible, but make sure that they are aware of the need to engage the parent

in tactful, diplomatic and above all, confidential conversation about their child.

- Remind the parent(s) that you value their perspective and want to work with them in helping their child make good progress and development.

- If the parent continues to find it hard to accept your concerns, you may want to direct them to a local parent support /parent partnership agency while you work with the SENCo to address the child's needs.

- Remember that a child's health and wellbeing is inextricably linked with that of their parents' and a stressed, angry or anxious parent is not in the best position to help their child.

- However, you also have a responsibility to use your professional judgement in the best interests of the child and a parent may not always agree with you.

If you are concerned about a child's development and progress, always gather observations and additional evidence as well as seeking advice from managers, childminder support officers, SENCo and other professionals within local children service teams, the health service or where relevant, voluntary organisations and agencies.

Measuring and assessing growth and development

There are now formal ways of sharing progress with parents/carers at different stages in the EYFS. Currently, the Progress Check at Two focuses on the Prime areas and the EYFS Profile is completed at the end of the Early Years Foundation Stage before a child transfers to Y1.

The Progress Check at Two

Statutory Requirements

2.3 When a child is aged between two and three, practitioners must review their progress, and provide parents and/or carers with a short written summary of their child's development in the prime areas.

There is no prescribed format for the written summary of the Progress Check at Two. The National Children's Bureau has produced guidance which includes examples of formats and case studies. The key principles describe how the check:

- should be completed by a practitioner who knows the child well and works directly with them in

the setting. This should normally be the child's key person;

- arises from the ongoing observational assessments carried out as part of everyday practice in the setting;

- is based on skills, knowledge, understanding and behaviour that the child demonstrates consistently and independently;

- takes account of the views and contributions of parents;

- takes into account the views of other practitioners and, where relevant, other professionals working with the child;

- enables children to contribute actively to the process.

From *A Know How Guide: The EYFS Progress Check at Age Two* (March 2012).

These are important principles to ensure that the check and the methods by which it is completed do not have a negative impact on the wellbeing of children and their families.

In particular, they promote the concept of 'listening to children' and valuing their contributions to the process.

Early Years Foundation Stage Profile

Statutory Requirements

2.6 In the final term of the year in which the child reaches age five, and no later than 30 June in that term, the EYFS Profile must be completed for each child. The Profile provides parents and carers, practitioners and teachers with a well-rounded picture of a child's knowledge, understanding and abilities, their progress against expected levels, and their readiness for Year 1.

The EYFS Profile provides a summary of a child's attainment at the end of the EYFS, based on ongoing observation and assessment of the 17 Early Learning Goals ranged across the prime and specific areas of learning.

The prime areas of learning

- communication and language
- physical development
- personal, social and emotional development

The specific areas of learning

- literacy
- mathematics
- understanding the world
- expressive arts and design

The handbook for the EYFS profile (available online at www.gov.uk) states that:

- Assessments will be based primarily on observation of daily activities and events.

- Practitioners should note in particular the learning which a child demonstrates spontaneously, independently and consistently in a range of contexts.

- Accurate assessment will take account of a range of perspectives including those of the child, parents and carers and other adults who have significant interactions with the child.

- For each Early Learning Goal, practitioners must judge whether a child is meeting the level of development expected at the end of the Reception Year (expected), exceeding this level (exceeding), or not yet reaching this level (emerging).

Practitioners are also reminded that they should make

sure that the provision enables all children, regardless of their stage of development or interests, needs and inclinations, to demonstrate attainment in ways that are motivating to them.

Both the Progress Check at Two and the EYFS Profile are summative assessments in that they provide a snapshot of a child at a particular stage. Formative or ongoing individual assessments will contribute not just to these checks, but also to the planning for each individual child. Observations are at the heart of this and provide the most effective way of reflecting on a child's wellbeing.

Partnership with parents

Involving parents in the assessment process is, of course, very important. Regular, ongoing discussion and sharing of children's progress and development ensures a full and rounded picture of the child.

Regular, relaxed and informal opportunities for sharing concerns and celebrating progress provide reassurance for all parents and particularly those who may be more anxious or worried. Arrived at in partnership, there should be nothing in the Progress Check or Profile that comes as a surprise or alarms parents.

(Both the *Handbook for the Early Years Profile* and the *NCB Know How Guide: The EYFS Progress Check at Age Two* are available to download as pdfs from www.gov.uk)

Assessing health and wellbeing

> ### Statutory Requirements
>
> 3.1 Children learn best when they are healthy, safe and secure, when their individual needs are met, and when they have positive relationships with the adults caring for them.

Practitioners are not formally asked to specifically check or measure health and wellbeing, although commenting on the prime areas and the characteristics of effective learning provides opportunity for this. Evidence increasingly suggests that wellbeing in the early years may be a predictor of later development and learning, so it makes sense to consider making assessment of wellbeing an integral feature of formative assessment for planning and future learning. Ferre Laevers, working in Belgium at the University of Leuven, has produced the Leuven Scales of Wellbeing and Involvement which are increasingly being used in the UK. The scales help practitioners better understand the levels of a child's wellbeing and their involvement with the learning environment. Laevers makes the point that both wellbeing and involvement are necessary for learning to take place and that the scales help practitioners to make assessments of the quality of their provision for each child. If an assessment shows that a child has poor wellbeing and/or involvement then the setting must address what needs to be done to improve the quality of care and education for that child.

It is particularly important that assessments for children with special educational needs and disability (SEND), should include reference to their wellbeing. These children and their parents are regularly subject to assessments and investigations into their progress, that inevitably focus on what they struggle with or are unable to achieve. It is essential that the child's wellbeing is reviewed regularly, to make sure that the environment, especially in a mainstream setting, is in tune with their emotional as well as their physical needs.

Observation and paying attention to children

> *'The quality of our observation depends primarily on the quality of attention that we give to the children we are observing'.* (Roberts 2010).

Observation is at the heart of early years assessment – and essential if we are to gain any real insight into a child's development and wellbeing. Through observation and careful listening we learn to pay particular attention to the many ways children share their own sense of their wellbeing with us. A rich and effective observation isn't always a lengthy narrative. Sometimes just a few key words will remind us of something we have seen that tells us about several different aspects of a child's development including their confidence, curiosity, self awareness, or persistence, as well as a problem solved in the block corner or a new maths concept acquired. Written up later, an observation makes a good starting point for a conversation with a parent and a trigger for planning as well as evidence for a Progress Check or later Profile. (Roberts 2010).

Rosemary Roberts, in her book *Wellbeing from Birth* comments on the way that good observation isn't just about outcomes i.e. noticing what a child did, how they did it, when they did it and why they did it – although these have their uses.

She describes the interactive process of observation and how children benefit from the specific attention gained from being observed, even if nothing more than a smile is shared in acknowledgement of what the practitioner saw taking place. She describes this as 'companionable attention' and believes it plays an important part in children's learning as well as their wellbeing.

> *'When observation is an interactive process of companionable attention, it not only gives us the material that we need for purposes such as planning, or reporting, or accountability – it actually is the work of companionable learning. Companionable attention is how we make relationships with children, so that we know what support they need in order to learn. It is an important factor in how young children's wellbeing thrives'.* (Roberts 2010).

Assessing children for whom English is an additional language

> ### Statutory Requirements
>
> 1.8 For children whose home language is not English, providers must take reasonable steps to provide opportunities for children to develop and use their home language in play and learning, supporting their language development at home.

Observation is essential for practitioners working with children for whom English is an additional language. They will all be at different stages of learning English as well as one (or maybe more) home languages. As the EYFS framework points out, it is essential to gather as much information as possible about the child's language use at home. Parents need to be reassured and encouraged to appreciate that development in the child's first language also helps their developing English, so it is desirable that they should continue to use it both at home and in the setting. Observation and discussion with parents and/ or bilingual assistants, where possible, is the key to being confident about what the child really knows and understands. The framework makes it very clear that children need to be able to engage in activities that do not depend solely on their level of English for success. They must be able to participate in activities in ways that will reveal what they know and can do in the security of their home language.

The impact of assessment on health and wellbeing

We are in a time when government understanding of quality in care and education rests mostly on data and target setting and when there have been constant changes to policies and guidelines. Early years practitioners have done their best to ensure that these demands don't affect the wellbeing of children and families although more baseline assessments will add to the pressures. To use the old analogy of the farmer who spent more time weighing his pig than he did feeding it – we are in danger of spending more time 'weighing' children with assessments and paperwork than we are in 'feeding' them with good quality care and play experiences.

Despite this, early years practitioners who are resourceful and resilient, who believe strongly in a pedagogy rooted in child development and experiential approaches will continue to use observation as their main form of assessment and ensure that children's wellbeing is safeguarded, whilst policies come and go.

Transitions and wellbeing

A key function of assessment is to provide information about a child and their progress as they move to a new setting or stages within settings.

Vertical and horizontal transitions

As children grow and develop they are faced with a range of transitions, large and small, some of which they seem to sail through, but all can affect their wellbeing. The transition from home to nursery or school is considered one of the major transitions in a child's life and yet, in recent times, a child may typically have already experienced several transitions by the time they make the move to school.

The possibilities are varied, ranging from 'in home care' with a nanny/au pair or family member to 'out of home care' with a childminder, or in a day care setting, at toddler group, crèche, nursery, pre-school, and finally to school, all before the age of five.

The transitions that mark the big changes over time, from year to year, e.g. from home, to a nursery class for a year and then to school, are called vertical transitions. But some children will experience several changes of setting during their day or their week, such as going from home to childminder, then to nursery, back to childminder and then home again. These are described as horizontal transitions. We must also be mindful of all the little changes experienced by a baby or young child during their day. Maybe they have to move from one room to another, staying in the setting while practitioners change shifts? Perhaps a favoured toy or activity might be casually cleared up and moved out of sight, not to reappear until the following week. There are big events too, like Christmas parties or the school photographer arriving, that shift routines all around. The kinds of transitions that often go unnoticed by adults, such as moving from the classroom to the dinner room, or from the big playground back inside again, sometimes present 4 year olds in reception classes with challenges to their wellbeing that are unsettling and can often lead to disruptive behaviour.

Something to think about

○ How do your admissions and transition procedures reflect a concern for the physical and emotional well-being of children and their families during the process?

○ How do you monitor wellbeing during transition and settling?

○ How do you support children's friendships particularly at times of transition?

○ New admissions and the responsibilities of settling children can also take their toll on practitioners' wellbeing. What support do practitioners need during the settling and transition process to ensure they can be fully attentive and available to children, particularly if they are balancing the needs of other children as well as those who are new.

○ How do you personally cope with change? How does it relate to your experiences of transition?

What can we do to support children's wellbeing during transitions

Practitioners need to make sure that as much information as possible is shared with them, from home and any other settings that already know the child. Some of that information may change depending on the age of the child, but some features are always vitally important.

● Make sure you can accurately pronounce (and spell) their name and that of their parent(s) and carers.

● Learn about their likes and interests, what motivates and interests them, but also find out the triggers for anxious or challenging behaviours and what strategies will soothe and calm them.

● Find out what transitional objects /routines will help them through the settling process and how you can help them 'hold their family in mind' while they are away from them. (See Section 3 for more about being 'held in mind'.)

Remember too, that their parent(s) will also be going through transition and may need support to safeguard their wellbeing during the change. Children and parents will have their own unique ways of handling transition, so pay careful attention during settling periods just as much to what they don't say (or do) as to what they may choose to tell you.

Transitions and attachment

It might be thought that children cope better with transitions if they don't become too attached to their carers. Work with adopted and fostered children has shown the opposite to be true. Children with secure attachments to one or more key carers, who know they are loved – and are loveable – and have had the benefit of a secure base from which to go out and explore new things, tend to handle transitions more ably than children with insecure attachments, who haven't formed strong connections with carers and struggle with change.

Some children seem to cope very well at first, only to have an unexpected dip in their wellbeing sometime later. Often referred to as the 'honeymoon period', it is easy to think it is just a case of the novelty having worn off. But it is possible that the child is experiencing a delayed reaction to the separation from familiar people and places. Elinor Goldschmied and Sonia Jackson (1994) compared this to the delayed shock that often occurs after a bereavement, when something small can trigger a huge sense of sadness in the child, as they experience again the emotions of separation distress.

Some children may seem to be handling the transition well in the setting, but at home they might display regressive behaviours such as clinginess, bedwetting or behaviours that are out of character, as they process the difficulties of change, at home in a familiar and safe environment.

Be sensitive to parents' feelings – it doesn't help to be told 'we don't have any problems with her when she's here' when your usually happy little girl is behaving badly at home – particularly if the reason for the change in behaviour is because she is exhausted from trying to be 'good' all day at her new nursery. Similarly, think how it feels for a parent to have left their child crying with a new carer only to be told, "she was fine when you left". How much nicer to hear "she missed you but then she found a friend to play with and soon felt better"? (O'Connor 2012).

Children who are extra vulnerable during times of change, such as 'Looked After' and adopted children, will need careful attention before, during and potentially long after a transition has occurred. For these children coming back after the weekend can be like starting all over again, given the fragility of their emotional security. September will probably always be a traumatic time for them, as year after year it signals yet another transition as they change classes, teachers and sometimes friendship groups, all of which can trigger traumatic memories. Friends are a major form of support for all children during transitions, and an important source of stability and security when facing new experiences. Most of us, as adults, would probably choose to have a friend or partner with us when facing change and the feelings can be even more intense for young children. As much as possible, consider children's friendship groups when organising transitions both big and small.

CASE STUDY: TOO SOON?

Safia was due to start at her nursery class just after she was 3. She seemed happy to meet the practitioners on the home visit, although she stayed shyly by mum's knee the whole time.

Her father stayed with her for the first week, and the sessions were kept to a minimum of one hour or so.

On the second week of settling, the plan was for Dad to leave the room for a few minutes, but Safia started to cry every time he tried to leave. When he did manage to leave, Safia's screams could be heard throughout the building. Nothing would console her even when Dad came back.

Each day for several weeks Dad would leave the room for only a short time and Safia would scream and cry inconsolably. She refused to leave dad's side whilst he was there and wouldn't make eye contact with either of her key people.

Between them they had a great deal of experience settling children and both agreed that Safia's reluctance was out of the ordinary.

They discussed with the family the possibility of delaying her start in nursery for another six months, with the proviso that she and dad pop in every so often just to say hello.

Six months later Safia came back to nursery and within a week was happy to let Dad go home, while she stayed for the morning by herself. Within a couple of months she was happily staying for the full day.

Ask yourself:
- What do you think made the difference to Safia's ability to eventually settle?
- Should the practitioners have persevered with her settling?
- What if the parents had not been in a position to delay her start at nursery?

Checklist

If your setting promotes healthy growth and development you will see children who:

- thrive and flourish regardless of any additional needs;

- whose milestones are monitored, allowing for individual rates of growth and development;

- are given appropriate support during optimal times of development;

- are provided with a stimulating and nurturing environment;

- contribute to assessments of their progress and offer opinions on their likes and dislikes, motivations and interests;

- are comfortable using their first language with adults and other children and feel confident in experimenting and demonstrating their growing abilities in English;

- are interested in the languages spoken by others and enjoy using new vocabulary and songs, rhymes etc. in a variety of languages;

- are supported through daily transitions as well as major life changes, with sensitivity and knowledge of how best to settle individual children and support their families.

You will see practitioners who:

- are aware of the impact of pre-natal and early life experiences on a child's development and that a child's wellbeing is strongly linked with that of their parents and family;

- use observation to create formative assessments leading to well informed summative assessments at required ages;

- are committed and enthusiastic about their role as key people and are skilled at 'tuning in' to babies and young children;

- respond to young children's needs as individuals rather than cohorts of children working at designated 'stages' of development, or in 'ability' groups;

- are aware of and respond to the particular needs of children in respect of their birthdates and how it affects admission dates etc. They use this information to sensitively differentiate and adjust expectations

where appropriate, whilst remaining open-minded about a child's individual potential, regardless of chronological age;

- understand the importance of the Prime areas of early childhood development;

- share concerns with parents in a sensitive, considerate manner, providing extra support where needed, to help parents understand specific issues;

- ensure assessments don't have a negative impact on children's wellbeing;

- understand and recognise indicators of abuse and neglect and the procedures involved in safeguarding children;

- appreciate the importance of both horizontal and vertical transitions on a child's wellbeing;

- take care to monitor their own levels of wellbeing and seek help and guidance when needed, particularly during periods of transition;

- have access to high quality training and supervision to ensure all the above.

and you will see parents who:

- feel relaxed and comfortable in the setting;

- have a good relationship with their child's key person(s) based on regular informal interactions;

- receive regular information about their child's progress and development, along with incidental news about their child's day in the setting;

- know that any concerns will be raised with them at an early stage, with sensitivity and consideration and that they will be signposted to other agencies etc. for further help and guidance if needed;

- will be helped with transitions, involved in decisions about 'settling in' periods, and made comfortable and welcomed in the setting when they stay with their children to help settle them.

Section 2:
Physical wellbeing

EYFS Unique child Card 1:4 Growing and developing

○ Physical well-being includes the growth and physical development of babies and children.

○ They have a biological drive to use their physical skills and benefit from physical activity.

○ Remember that children gain control of their bodies gradually.

Activity and movement

This 'biological drive' to use their bodies and their developing physical skills referred to in the EYFS Themes and Commitments (2008) is fundamental, not just to

the growth of muscles and joints, but also to brain development. Because of the link between physical development and the architecture of the brain, we refer to this specifically as neurophysiological development.

Physical activity is vital long before a baby begins walking and moving around independently. Even in the womb, a foetus is moving and as well as helping to build their skeletal development those little kicks and movements are also the first language the child has for communicating with the world

Examples of some early primitive reflexes adapted from Pound (2013) and Goddard Blyth (2005)

The Moro Reflex

- The first of the primitive reflexes to emerge in the womb
- A response to a sudden unexpected event particularly where there is loss of support to the head and the head drops below the level of the spine
- The arms and legs open out, and with a sharp intake of breath the baby freezes for a second, before returning arms and legs in across the body, and protesting with a cry
- Provides a 'fail safe mechanism' for triggering a baby's first breath if they don't do it spontaneously by themselves
- Also triggers an arousal mechanism to activate a fight, flight or freeze reaction in response to perceived threat
- By about 4 months it should become gradually modified into a 'startle' response that allows the child to respond or ignore the alert

If the reflex stays active

- There can be increased sensitivity and overreaction to unexpected stimuli
- Increases the likelihood of a fight, flight or freeze reaction
- Doesn't allow time for conscious thought to analyse a situation before acting
- This reflex might be present in a child who is always in trouble for impulsive or inappropriate behaviour

The Spinal Galant Reflex

- Exists in the womb to help with the birth process and should be inhibited by around 9 months of age
- The skin on either side of the lower spine is sensitive to touch, causing the hip to flex on one side, while the other side arches in the opposite direction
- Making the hips flexible in this way, helps the baby negotiate their way through the birth canal
- It may also be linked to urinary and intestinal function
- It should become gradually inhibited over the first 9 months of life, when babies have lots of opportunities to lie on their backs, kicking and wriggling

If the reflex stays active

- It can cause hypersensitivity in the lower back and the slightest touch can activate it
- This can make it very difficult for a child (or adult) to sit still
- This reflex might be still present in a child who is always in trouble for fidgeting and not sitting still
- It might also be linked to bedwetting

Symmetrical Tonic Neck Reflex (STNR)

- Active for a short period after birth and then returns at 6-9 months
- Should become inhibited at 9-11 months
- Makes upper and lower body perform opposite movements
- Helps the baby get ready to crawl by bending the arms and straightening the legs when the head goes down
- When the head goes back up, the arms straighten, the legs bend and the bottom sinks back down
- Weight bearing on hands and knees helps align upper and lower ends of spine ready for standing
- Helps train visual adjustment from near to far (looking down at the ground and up/out into the distance)

If the reflex stays active

- Can cause poor hand-eye coordination
- Problems with movements involving upper and lower body co-ordination e.g. swimming
- This reflex might still be present in a child who is a messy eater, has poor posture or can't sit still and upright at a table

outside the womb. Once born, we expect a baby to wriggle and squirm, to kick their legs and reach out with their hands, without realising that every time a movement Is repeated it is creating and reinforcing an important pathway in the brain.

Primitive reflexes

There is an another important reason for all those kicks and wriggles. We are all born with 'primitive reflexes' that exist in the womb and are vital for our survival and in our earliest months. A reflex is an involuntary response usually to a stimulus of some kind.

Because a reflex action is involuntary, it is hard to suppress while it is still active, but it can become 'inhibited', which means it is no longer as responsive to the stimulus.

Once we are born, these primitive reflexes need to be inhibited so that they don't interfere with our physical development outside the womb and beyond the first six months of life. The best way for this to happen is through lots of spontaneous, natural physical activity, usually when being held or lying on backs or tummies. Unlike most baby animals, baby humans can't get up and stand on their feet and walk around straight away. Ideally, we spend our first twelve months (or so) being held and cuddled, rocked and dandled as well as lying on our tummies and backs with our legs and arms free to kick and wave. Then we learn to roll over and start to creep and crawl before we pull ourselves up and start to toddle about and begin to walk. Walking is seen as a very important milestone in a baby's life, but in truth, it is the activity that happens before walking that is hugely important in our physical development, and is particularly significant in the inhibition of those primitive reflexes.

Creeping and crawling

The interaction with the ground or other flat surfaces, when they are playing on their backs or tummies allows many of the opportunities babies and children need to inhibit their primary reflexes.

For most babies, after they have managed to roll over, there is a period of time when they begin to pull themselves along the floor, first with their bellies low down and then up on their hands and knees (or feet). This process is more than just an 'in between' stage before walking begins. It is a vital part of early physical growth and has an important part to play in many aspects of a child's development, including neurological, visual, co-ordination and spatial development. In the 'Well-Balanced Child' (2005) Sally Goddard Blythe also suggests that the early physical development of infants matches our understanding of evolutionary development. As well as providing a blue print for the development of locomotion, the theory also emphasises the importance of each one of these early stages as more than just a stepping stone on the way to the ultimate goal of walking.

First, the child is in a fish-like state in the womb, then a 'reptilian' stage when they begin creeping on their tummies and raising their heads, followed by the 'mammalian' stage of crawling around on hands and knees/feet. Once they begin pulling themselves up to stand and cruise round the furniture, or walk holding someone's hands, they are at the 'primate' stage where their arms and hands are still fundamental to their mobility, before finally they reach the 'human' bipedal stage where they can move speedily in a variety of ways leaving their hands free to do other things at the same time.

Tummy time

Time spent on the tummy is really beneficial to babies and young children. Just a few carefully supervised minutes on a lap, a blanket on the floor or even outdoors on the grass in good weather, is the first step to an important physical development 'workout' that has many long term benefits.

Time on the tummy:

- helps lengthen the spine and develop the neck muscles

- expands the chest cavity, allowing for deeper breathing

- allows weight bearing through the hands which develops a full palm stretch – important for finger dexterity, strength of grip and fine motor skills

- encourages close range eye focusing

- decreases primitive reflexes that tie head movement to whole body movement

- helps body alignment by freeing the head to move separately from the body

- begins to develop movement across the mid-line of the body, which create the cross-lateral connections thought to be important for higher level thinking and memory skills.

Racing to walk

Typically, children begin to walk anytime between 9 and 15 months. There have always been children who are early walkers, and it is human nature to encourage and applaud the moment a child begins to walk. It is seen as a major milestone in a child's life, is often recorded and is a question regularly asked in infant health checks. We know that delayed walking might be an indicator of problems with development, though not always. But we also have evidence now to suggest that some children who walk early and miss out on crawling may have later difficulties with some aspects of co-ordination (such as understanding left and right); visual difficulties (copying from a board); and other neurological issues that can interfere with cognitive development. This is not to suggest that children should be prevented from walking early or made to crawl when they are reluctant but as Sally Goddard Blythe (2005) reminds us, 'The important point is to allow your baby to experience as wide a range of movements as possible; to enjoy and value each stage of development as it occurs'.

Why might children miss out on some of these neurophysiological stages?

There are a variety of reasons why children might spend less time on their backs or tummies, or crawling around on the floor in the way they have done in the past.

chest space and developing both long and close vision as they look first at the floor and then out in front of them.

Some babies and children don't like being put on their tummies so parents are reluctant to try. It is important to be sensitive to what the individual child can handle, but there are safe and gentle ways to make the sensation more fun and enjoyable, gradually building up their tolerance.

3. Adult attitudes to risk

In these health and safety conscious times, some children have become more restricted in their play experiences tending to spend more time indoors watching TV and playing screen based games. They have fewer opportunities for rough and tumble games and for playing outdoors, stretching, climbing, rolling and sliding etc.

Why does it matter?

Statutory Requirements

The moving and handling aspect of the ELG for Physical development requires that: children show good control and co-ordination in large and small movements. They move confidently in a range of ways, safely negotiating space. They handle equipment and tools effectively, including pencils for writing. (EYFS Framework 2012).

A study of reception age children in Sutton Coldfield in 2012 was the first to measure foundation stage children's neuromotor skills against their performance at school. Its findings were that children who struggle to sit still or hold a pencil, may not have fully completed steps in their neurophysiological development as babies (www.open-doors-therapy.co.uk).

It seems there 'are children who are 5 year olds on the outside, but three year olds in terms of their motor skills'. (Goddard Blythe, 2011). This has a major impact, not only on the health and wellbeing of the individual child, but also to generations of children whose potential is being compromised by cultural and lifestyle changes. What makes it worse is that these children are prematurely deemed to be 'failing' and 'unready' for school when, more often than not, they have been denied the physical experiences necessary to develop the required motor skills. This has a knock on effect on their self esteem, their confidence and ultimately their sense of wellbeing. Research by early years movement specialists, Jabadao, over a ten year period is beginning to show the positive impact of movement activity on children's emotional wellbeing.

1. A change in the way we move babies around

Think about how much time a baby or small child is likely to spend in a baby seat of one form or another – in a car/ at home or strapped into a buggy. There are good safety reasons for these obviously, and for car seats in particular, but today's lifestyle often means that children spend a lot of time in them, even staying in the car seat when they are transferred indoors. Buggies are undeniably more convenient, but they don't provide the opportunities to lie down in the way that old-style prams did. It is unrealistic to think that we should turn back time, but we must be aware of the implications of progress in 'transporting' children around. We need to consider how we can make up for the amount of time children spend sitting curled in a 'c' shape rather than being carried in loving arms or lying on their backs, kicking and wriggling on the floor or in a pram.

2. A reluctance to put babies on their tummies

As a result of new awareness of the potential causes of Sudden Infant Death Syndrome (SIDS) parents are advised not to let their babies sleep on their tummies. This seems to have led to generalised public anxiety about putting babies on their fronts at other times when they are awake. This has meant that babies and young children are missing out on valuable time spent (supervised) on their tummies, strengthening their neck and arm muscles, opening their

How we can help children with their physical development

- we can provide lots of opportunities for physical play and movement

- these can be in specific movement sessions but also encouraged in the way that the learning environment is organised both indoors and out

- we can encourage children down on to the floor for crawling experience, tummy time activities and general floor play indoors and out

- put games and activities down on the floor to encourage older children

- have circle or story times down on your tummies

Make the most of the floor for activities and learning opportunities.

Sensory integration

Also playing a significant role in neurophysiological development is the sensory system.

'Sensations are 'food' or nourishment for the nervous system. Every muscle, joint, vital organ, bit of skin, and sense organ in the head sends sensory inputs to the brain. Every sensation is a form of information. The nervous system uses this information to produce responses that adapt the body and mind to that information. The brain needs a continuous variety of sensory nourishment to develop and then to function'. (Ayres 1980).

We tend to think of 5 senses: sight, sound, smell, taste and touch. Strictly speaking these are the sensations that come from the senses: the visual, the olfactory, the auditory, the gustatory and the tactile senses. These are the exteroceptors – the sensations that provide information on what is outside our bodies. But from a neurophysiological perspective, there are two further sensory systems that play a huge role in our daily lives and are significant in our physical and emotional wellbeing. These are the proprioceptors – the sensations that tell us where our bodies are in space and how they are moving.

The proprioceptive sense

This provides sensory information about our movements, and though the information comes from our muscles and joints, it is largely subconscious because most of it is processed in parts of the brain that don't have conscious awareness. Proprioception helps us to move without having to think about how we do it – it is what helps us walk downstairs, get into a car or tie our hair up without having to think about it or look at what we are doing. Children build proprioception through movement, which is why they need plenty of opportunities to move. When proprioception is underdeveloped or 'poorly organised', a person has to rely much more on visual information by looking very closely at what the body is doing. Children with poor proprioception tend to be 'clumsier' and find it difficult to do things if they can't see with their eyes what their body is doing. This might be why some children find it difficult to sleep on their own or in the dark – they need

Something to think about

O How do you support parents to appreciate the value of physical activity and movement in their child's first years?

O How well do you think educators and other professionals understand the role of primitive reflexes in general development and future learning? How can you help them appreciate the importance of recognising them in assessment of children's later learning difficulties?

CASE STUDY: MOVEMENT SPACE

After having heard Penny Greenland speak at an Early Education Conference (Life in Every Limb 2012), a reception class teacher created a movement space in an area of her classroom.

She put four PE mats in a corner where there would be the least interference from other furniture and resources. As advised, she made sure that it was used purely for movement and not for any other activity (e.g. doubling up as a block area, or book corner). There was only one rule – that the children should remove their shoes.

She was amazed not just at how sensibly they used the space – but also how inventive they were. Observing the children, she saw them developing sophisticated movements similar to ballet or yoga and collaborating to produce dances as well as engaging in 'robust' play with all the positive elements of rough and tumble but safely contained on the mats.

Over time, she has seen improvements in children's physical development as well as a reduction in behavioural issues.

The teacher values the impact the physical area has on children's wellbeing and has created a similar space with her current class, explaining its use and purpose to parents at their initial meeting. She intends to always make it as much a part of her continuous provision as her book corner!

Ask yourself:
- What would you need to do to create an indoor movement area?
- What do you think would be the main challenges?
- How would you support parents and other adults to appreciate the benefits of it?
- How would you use observations from the area to support your assessments of children? How would you feel about joining in yourself with the physical play on the mats and encouraging other adults to have a go?

physical contact with someone else to help them feel safe at night and the darkness overwhelms them because they can't see themselves.

The vestibular sense

The vestibular sense provides the sensory information that tells us about our head movement, balance and relationship with gravity. This is linked to the inner ear and two types of vestibular receptors. One responds to gravity – and is continually sending 'a perpetual stream of vestibular messages throughout one's entire life'. (Ayres 2005). The other type of receptor is linked to our head movements, and picks up information from the pressure of the fluid in the ear canals. The combination of both of these kinds of input is extremely precise and tells us important information such as:

- where am I in relation to gravity?

- am I standing still or moving?

- how fast am I going?

- what direction am I going in?

This is not like having a speedometer or a map – it is much more basic – and subtle – than that. So basic that we take it for granted that our brain is processing all of this information.

The vestibular receptors are incredibly sensitive so that even the most subtle changes in movement or position are registered in the brain. We are seldom aware of them, unless we stimulate them intensely, e.g. spinning, riding in a roller coaster. Even when we suffer motion sickness or vertigo, we feel the sensations in our bodies rather than in our ears.

It's also the system for unifying all sorts of other sensations from outside and inside the body, which are processed in reference to the basic information coming from the vestibular sense. 'The activity in the vestibular system provides a framework for the other aspects of our experience. Vestibular input seems to "prime" the entire nervous system to function effectively'. (Ayres 2005).

Children instinctively know this, seeking out activities, such as spinning, rolling, sliding, swinging etc., that stimulate the vestibular system – and adults instinctively know this too as we gently rock children to sleep or stimulate them by throwing them up in the air and catching them safely! We turn them upside down and swing them gently, we sit them on our knees and let them fall through like 'Humpty Dumpty' and we play rough and tumble games that involve rolling around with squeals of mutual delight and laughter.

Sensory processing difficulties

This is all good news when it is working well, but there may be serious consequences for health and wellbeing when the sensory information isn't being processed properly. This is sometimes known as sensory processing disorder but is more accurately referred to as Sensory Integrative Dysfunction. (Ayres 2005). This is different to a sensory impairment. A child who is deaf, for example, receives little or no aural information – this is a lack of sensory input, not a lack of sensory integration. A child can have excellent hearing, but if the sensory information they receive from their ears does not have clear meaning, then they may have problems with comprehension and other areas of learning. Ayres and other neurophysiological experts believe that many learning and emotional difficulties may be the result of problems with sensory integration.

Traffic jam in the brain!

Ayres suggests that a simple way of understanding sensory processing is to think of the brain as a big city with all the neural impulses (sensory information) flowing like traffic through it. When the sensory processing is working well, the traffic flows easily and gets to its destination quickly. When it isn't, then there is a big traffic jam in the brain. Some bits of

information get through but certain parts of the brain don't get any of the information they need to do their jobs properly.

We don't yet fully understand what causes this traffic jam in the brain although there are some possible factors that may contribute to sensory processing difficulties. We know that children whose early years were very deprived or neglectful, with little healthy stimulation through touch and contact with others are much less likely to develop adequate sensory, motor or intellectual functioning.

However, many children with sensory integrative dysfunction did not experience deprivation in their early lives and there appears no obvious reason for their difficulties. Indeed their difficulties may not even be recognised as anything other than challenging behaviour or learning delay, with the expectation that the child has some control over their abilities, behaviour or attainment and just has to work harder and behave better. Improved awareness of the importance of neurophysiological development and sensory processing issues gives us a new framework for understanding a child's puzzling behaviours. This should hopefully bring better outcomes for children, as well as more support for their parents and the practitioners who work with them.

Sensory Integrative Dysfunction

Some common signs of Sensory Integrative Dysfunction include:

- hyperactivity/distractibility – constantly moving, seems unable to be still, struggles to shut out other distractions in order to concentrate, seems 'all over the place', loses things

- behaviour problems – more fussy/things are never right, less happy, hates to lose, has difficulties with sharing, overly sensitive, struggles with change and even low levels of stress

- speech and language delay – poor articulation and late speech development

- muscle tone and co-ordination difficulties – weakness, tires easily, prefers to lean when standing and rest head on arms when sitting, poor motor coordination, loses balance easily, drops things more often than usual, clumsy movements, finds things like blocks and puzzles a challenge

- poor spatial awareness – bumps into people and things, struggles to copy things off a board

- learning difficulties – reading and writing may present specific challenges.

Sensory Integrative Dysfunction can have a huge impact on wellbeing, particularly when the difficulties above go unnoticed or are misunderstood. Furthermore, the vestibular system, being strongly linked with balance and equilibrium, is important for emotional stability just as much as physical balance. Just think of the many ways we use the words 'balanced' and 'stable' to describe a person's mental state. (Goddard Blyth 2005).

Importance of touch

Ayres described the tactile, vestibular and proprioceptive functions as 'building blocks for emotional security', highlighting touch as a 'primal source of comfort'. (Ayres 2005). Our sense of touch is strongly linked with our emotions right from the beginning, as positive experiences and attachment with our caregivers rely on gentle, loving touch.

Some children can be soothed with a little stroking, or just the calm touch of an adult sitting beside them. Others will demand (and give) strong bear hugs. Some children may not register, or moderate, the strength of their touch and others may resist being touched altogether. Tactile defensiveness may indicate a problem with sensory integration, so pay attention to a child's tolerance for touch and always seek advice and guidance if you are concerned. As with other sensory processing difficulties, we do not always know the cause and it is important to state that most children with tactile issues were not neglected or deprived of positive touch. Make the most of opportunities for messy play for everyone. Playing with clay, sand, water and mud are good for building connections in the brain and integrating the senses.

How do we help children with Sensory Integrative Dysfunction?

We may not know much yet about the causes of Sensory Integration Dysfunction, but through the work of Dr. Ayres and others, and institutions such as INPP (Institute of Neurophysiological Pyschology – www.inpp.org.uk) we now have lots of strategies to support both adults and children with sensory-related physical and emotional issues and associated learning difficulties. Always seek advice from SENCos, management and other professionals if you have concerns about a child's sensory integration.

However, games and activities that stimulate and support the development of the vestibular and proprioceptive senses to create strong 'body maps' and help with 'motor planning' (praxis) are good news for everyone and are

easy to incorporate into continuous provision, as well as specific dance or PE sessions.

Here's just a few to try:

For proprioception:

- real work activities such as lifting and carrying, pushing and pulling, sweeping and scrubbing all help build proprioception

- cushions and blankets are great for rolling around in and making 'kid sandwiches' – these build body awareness

- rough and tumble play – this is good for both boys and girls and is valuable for many reasons, including physical problem solving. It is different from fighting and aggressive play in that all the participants can benefit from it (there are usually no winners and losers) and all are likely to feel 'good' after it. (LeVoguer and Pasch 2014).

With vestibular activities:

- be very sensitive to the child's age and development. Always 'check in' with children for their consent to the activity and watch for non verbal signals of body tension/relaxation to indicate whether they are comfortable with an activity

- swaying and rocking with a child in your arms or on your lap means you can perfectly judge their enjoyment levels and how far to take the activity

- gentle rocking, swaying, twirling, swinging, slow spinning and playing see saws and 'row row your boat' are good for under-threes. Older children like to increase speed and intensity, but remember to use gentle swaying and rocking also to soothe and focus attention. (Daly and O'Connor 2009). Enjoy a twirl or a spin yourself as you move around the setting and especially out in the garden. Children won't need much encouragement to mirror your actions!

Something to think about

- Why do you think we link 'balance' with emotional wellbeing and mental stability?

- Can you think of children whose sensory integration difficulties might have gone unrecognised in the past?

- Do you currently work with children whose behaviours are puzzling and don't respond to conventional behaviour management strategies?

Stimulation and language development

The brain needs sensory stimulation to grow and develop. Everything a child sees, hears, smells, tastes and touches helps build their brain architecture. Too little stimulation, particularly during the prime times of development means the brain doesn't get fired up enough to create lots of new pathways. But too much stimulation, of the wrong kind, at the wrong time is just as damaging. Babies can get very agitated if there is too much going on around them – but too little means their brains don't receive the input they need for language to develop, and for their social and emotional development. To get the amount of stimulation just right, they need adults who can 'tune into' them with just the right amount of stimulation to fire up their brains but not overload them. We still don't know the full effects of new technologies, so it would seem to make sense to be concerned about excessive use of 'screen time' with young children. For now, we can counteract it with plenty of opportunity for activities that we know do provide the right amount of developmentally healthy stimulation for communication and wellbeing.

There is widespread concern about young children's language development and it is easy to see how a lack of appropriate stimulation from the start of a child's life could have a negative impact. They need loving, interested people around them who can gauge verbal and non verbal communication to the right level, often through 'motherese' – a way of speaking using tone and repetition that is most attractive to babies' ears. Pusher facing buggies promote language and connection with carers, and routines and rituals during the day provide children with predictable language that they can draw on and extend their vocabulary.

Lack of vestibular activity has also been linked to language development as it encourages vocalisation (think how we scream on a roller coaster) and there is a concern that lack of vestibular activity in young children (e.g. vigorous play outdoors) may be a contributing factor to language delay in some children. Minimise the risk by providing lots of opportunity for exuberant outdoor play that promotes vocalising and the chance to shout and make noise.

Something to think about

O Can you think of children you work with whose challenging behaviours may be linked to a lack of healthy stimulation in their early lives?

O How does this information challenge or support you to respond appropriately to their behavioural needs?

Too soon for school readiness?

One aspect not addressed by the Sutton Coldfield research into motor skills, is whether or not the requirements for children to 'prove' their readiness for school in terms of their motor skills are in fact not somewhat out of tune with children's typical motor and sensory development. For some educationalists, school readiness at four flies in the face of the neurophysiological evidence that much of a child's neuromotor skills are not, in fact, fully developed until they are older. (Goddard Blyth 2012). Many of the fine motor skills, co-ordination and sensory processing required of formal learning – to hold a pencil, to copy from a board, to sit still for lengthy periods – cannot be acquired until there has been sufficient gross motor development. This requires space and opportunity for lots of movement and activity, indoors and out, as well as the chance to explore 'real work' such as lifting and carrying etc. Being able to comfortably sit still requires balance and yet the vestibulary system which enables this, is not fully developed until around the age of seven. Four year olds trying to get their bodies to sit quietly on the carpet or to stand in a line are not just using up valuable 'brain space' that leaves them with little scope for listening and concentrating, they are also wasting precious time.

As Jean Ayres wrote,

'Asking the Kindergarten child to learn reading before his brain is ready for this task will not only be unproductive, but will also take the child away from sensorimotor activities that his brain needs now in order to learn reading at a later age'. (Ayres 1980).

An additional perspective on this issue comes from David Whitebread and Sue Bingham, in their paper on School Readiness (2011). 'The problem is not that children are not ready for school, but that our schools are not ready for children.'

Understanding safety and risk

Statutory Requirements

3.1 Children learn best when they are healthy, safe and secure, when their individual needs are met, and when they have positive relationships with the adults caring for them. The safeguarding and welfare requirements, [ ] are designed to help providers create high quality settings which are welcoming, safe and stimulating, and where children are able to enjoy learning and grow in confidence.

Statutory Requirements

3.9 Providers must ensure that people looking after children are suitable to fulfil the requirements of their roles. Providers must have effective systems in place to ensure that practitioners, and any other person who is likely to have regular contact with children (including those living or working on the premises), are suitable.

Everyone working with young children has a responsibility to ensure their safety at all times. Children may spend a significant amount of their time in childcare settings and schools and rely on the adults around them for both emotional as well as physical safety (see Section 3 for more about emotional security).

- It is our responsibility to eliminate unacceptable risk and hazards to physical safety and to have a policy of risk assessment in place to assure this.

- Children and their parents should feel secure in the knowledge that the people working with them are 'suitable' in that they have the training and motivations to want the best for them and ensure necessary safety.

Something to think about

○ What age do you think children should start school?

○ Do you think Physical Development is more or less important than the other two prime areas?

○ How can we balance knowledge about children's need for physical development against pressure to formalise education at a younger age?

- The physical environment, its layout and systems of organisation must be regularly checked and reviewed to ensure that children's safety and wellbeing are always paramount.

But as Helen Bradford points out in the introduction to her book *The Wellbeing of Children Under Three*

'Feeling secure and happy and being able to thrive means, paradoxically, that children must also feel able to take risks appropriate to their stages of development: to explore, enquire and experiment as their knowledge and understanding of the environments they inhabit grows'. (Bradford 2012).

Far from keeping children safe, an environment that doesn't encourage a degree of risk-taking actually creates unsafe children. These are the children who never learn to think for themselves before attempting something risky, who don't see ahead where potential dangers lie and never develop the resilience and strategies that will keep them safe when there are no adults around to do it for them. Our real aim in ensuring children are 'safe enough' (Tovey 2014) is to equip them ultimately to manage their own risk assessment.

Moreover, it is the emotional security and safety felt and experienced by a child that supports and enables them to take measured physical risks (as well as challenging themselves mentally, socially and intellectually). This means knowing the difference between evaluating, eradicating or safeguarding hazards, like an ill-fitting carpet, broken glass or a step that is too high for toddlers to manage – and evaluating the height of climbing apparatus so that it provides the right amount of challenge, or checking that resources and equipment continue to offer appropriate stimulation.

This is why the best kind of equipment to support robust, physical play is open-ended, rather than fixed and static. For example, A-frames and planks that can be adjusted according to children's heights and abilities make for more stimulating and adaptable climbing opportunities than fixed climbing frames, which often require excessive supervision.

Fear of legislation

There is a tendency to blame an overly 'health and safety conscious' climate on the reduction of opportunities for risk taking in children. This is unhelpful as there are many children still alive and unharmed now as a result of improvements in public safety, who in the past might have suffered as a result of dangerous play environments and lack of supervision. A responsible attitude towards public and individual health and safety is strongly linked to our wellbeing and sense of security. Unfortunately, it is the fear of legislation that has influenced a lot of recent policy making, encouraging a climate of anxiety and over-caution. Therefore, it is very important that practitioners retain a balanced and professional understanding of health and safety restrictions, helping young children and their families appreciate the difference between avoidable hazards and acceptable levels of healthy risk.

Having a go

'Development Matters' reminds us that 'an effective learner' is someone who is 'willing to have a go' through:

- initiating activities

- seeking challenge

- showing a 'can do' attitude

- taking a risk, engaging in new experiences and learning by trial and error.

Helen Tovey refers to the benefits of 'adventurous play' in developing children's dispositions for persistence and to see problems as challenges to be embraced and enjoyed. She also makes the point that 'There is evidence that risk and challenge in a supportive environment is positively linked with emotional well-being, resilience, and mental health and that small mistakes and minor accidents can offer some protection against the negative effects of future failure'. (Tovey 2014).

Children who feel 'emotionally safe' are more likely to take what Bowlby (1988) referred to as 'excursions' away from the secure base of trusted adults who provide a 'safe haven' if things go wrong and accidents happen. These are distinctive features of secure attachment and are fundamental in enabling children to desire – and make the most of – new and challenging experiences. If we want to encourage a 'have a go' attitude in our children then we must first seek to build their sense of emotional security.

Risky behaviours

Some children will be more physically cautious than others. This may be for a variety of reasons, but can be connected to their sensory and neuromotor development. Lots of opportunity for physical play indoors and out, with supportive adults, should enable most children to acquire the proprioceptive and vestibular skills necessary to develop physical mastery and build their confidence. But be aware of children who may need more specific help and as well as working with parents, involve managers and SENCos in decisions about referrals for input from other agencies.

Some children may seem to have little regard for their safety and frequently engage in risky behaviour and activities. Sometimes, this is just a case of reinstating boundaries and providing sensitive containment or opportunities for teaching, e.g. road safety. Occasionally, it might be an indicator of a more serious concern. Some children with attachment difficulties, and other related conduct disorders may not have developed the neural pathways to enable them to see the consequences of their actions and think before they act. Their impulsivity is not deliberately 'naughty' behaviour, although it may well feel deliberately challenging.

Children who are 'Looked After' or have been under-developed regard for their safety as a result of early neglect, although others may be over cautious as a result of threatening experiences or having been the 'carer' for younger siblings. What is crucial for all these children is the sensitive attunement of key people who understand them and their needs, in order to begin to learn how to manage risk safely.

First aid

Statutory Requirements

3.24 At least one person who has a current paediatric first aid certificate must be on the premises at all times when children are present, and must accompany children on outings. First aid training must be local authority approved and be relevant for workers caring for young children. Childminders, and any assistant who might be in sole charge of the children for any period of time, must hold a current paediatric first aid certificate.

As well as being a statutory requirement, first aid training contributes to general health and wellbeing. As adults, feeling confident that we can manage basic first aid allows us to be more relaxed around children, confidently encouraging them

to stretch and challenge themselves physically. Adults who are anxious around physical play are less likely to provide stimulating environments and support children with the right amount of challenge to take their physical learning forward.

Personal care, illness and medicine

Health and personal care

Statutory Requirements

Children know the importance for good health of physical exercise, and a healthy diet, and talk about ways to keep healthy and safe. They manage their own basic hygiene and personal needs successfully, including dressing and going to the toilet independently.

Not only are the personal care routines of babies and young children important for their general health, they also provide carers with regular opportunities for the kinds of intimacy and bonding that contribute to their emotional wellbeing. This is one of the fundamental reasons for the key person approach which has at its core the need for consistency and warmth during personal care routines. Having a nappy changed by four different people in a day, all efficient, but in a hurry to move onto another task, might leave a baby clean and dry – but also stressed and unhappy.

Contrast that with the experience of a baby in a setting where either one of their two key people are available to change them over the course of the day, taking time for a cuddle, a sing-song or a little massage while they clean them up. This kind of interaction builds attachment and enables attunement, both of which play a large part in a child's wellbeing. (More about this in Section 3.) Even with older children, it is worth making the most of the opportunity for a soapy hand massage with a child who needs encouragement to wash their hands well, but will also benefit from the personal contact.

Children who have positive associations with basic hygiene and personal care routines are more likely to choose to continue with them as they grow older and able to do things for themselves. A balanced attitude to cleanliness and personal hygiene is ultimately desirable, where a child is comfortable with messy activities and the possibilities of getting dirty, but is also aware of the health and other implications of not cleaning up after themselves and the need for good personal care routines.

Hand washing and infection

According to Professor Sally Bloomfield, (of the International Scientific Forum on Home Hygiene) infectious disease has moved steadily back up the health agenda. Outbreaks of food borne disease (food poisoning); gut infections caused by the norovirus, (winter vomiting disease) and other organisms such as Staphylococcus aureus (MRSA) and Clostridium difficile (C difficile); and respiratory viruses, e.g. SARS and Avian Flu etc. which are increasingly resistant to antibiotics, have prompted a new emphasis on developing strategies for prevention and control.

We need to reduce infection *and* reduce the amount of antibiotics we use and at the same time, we also need to sustain normal exposure to our 'old friends – the microbes and organisms from our evolutionary past that help to keep us healthy. (Rook 2013). 'Targeted hygiene' practices allow for this by focusing not on frequent hand washing or obsessive cleanliness but on hand washing at the right times. Bloomfield (2014) suggests that hand washing must be done after:

● going to the toilet

● handling or caring for pet animals

● returning from outings

● handling raw meat

● changing nappy or soiled clothes

● using tissues or wipes

and before:

● handling/preparing food

● caring for babies and young children.

Modelling good practice

We all know how much children love to copy adults, so they need to see high standards of hygiene and personal care from us. Time spent modelling good hand washing is time well-spent. Choose a nursery rhyme to sing alongside a hand washing routine. This helps ensure that enough time is spent on each part of the hand.

Children also need to hear us talk about how self-care contributes to our wellbeing. How a wash or shower can make us feel more alert and ready for the day or how

a warm bath can soothe and relax. At the same time we need to be aware that these might be facilities not always regularly available to all children at home and that judgements about cleanliness may be socially or culturally biased by our own experiences and upbringing.

Ideally, in an EYFS setting, the toilets and sinks will be part of the learning environment, easily accessible to the children and observable by staff. Children need to feel safe going to the toilet, so that they use them readily and with confidence. Toilet anxiety at a young age can lead to long term physical and emotional difficulties with, in extreme cases, children refusing to eat or drink so that they don't have to use a toilet outside the home.

Doing it for themselves

As an early years practitioner, sometimes it can feel like you spend most of your day doing up buttons and zipping up coats, although the advent of velcro has at least brought some relief from all the tying of shoelaces! But we are also lucky to be involved in that wondrous stage when children start to want to do things for themselves. We use our knowledge of their individual stage of development to sensitively judge when to step back and allow them the time to persevere with a tricky zip – and when to step in to avoid too much frustration damaging their self-esteem. It may seem that an inordinate amount of our time is spent on these little things – but to the individual child they are just as important as any other kind of learning and make a big difference to their sense of self and their physical and emotional wellbeing.

As they grow older, giving a child a degree of choice, for example, on a spring day as to whether or not they need to wear a coat to stay warm outside, fosters their ability to tune into their own physical needs as well as acknowledging their sense of agency in looking after themselves. That's not to suggest that you won't still have to insist on coat wearing sometimes, but observing a child coming back inside for their coat because they know they feel chilly, is a significant step in increasing maturity and self help skills.

Health and Illness

The statutory requirements with regard to dealing with illness and medicine in early years settings are clearly set out in the EYFS framework. As with any serious accident or injury, registered providers must notify OFSTED within 14 days of any serious illness of a child in their care, and of the action taken.

Make sure your policies and procedures are clear, that all members of staff are familiar with them and they are shared with parents. These will include the procedure for taking care of a child who becomes unwell in the setting as well as policies on when to exclude children with infections etc. Have resource materials readily available, that describe the signs and symptoms of illness in babies and young children, so that staff have up to date knowledge about common infections and childhood illnesses.

If a child shows signs of being unwell, make sure you monitor them closely. Keep a record of the signs and symptoms that cause concern and any action taken, e.g. taking their temperature. Provide reassurance and keep them comfortable while they wait to be collected.

It should go without saying, that a child's dignity and wellbeing should be preserved during illness, particularly bouts of vomiting, diarrhoea or clothes soiling. Respond calmly and efficiently so that other children are reassured and less likely to make a 'drama' out of such incidents. We probably all have childhood memories of being embarrassed by the reactions of others at times like these, only adding to the distress of feeling unwell. Ideally, settings will have a clean, private space for changing children out of soiled clothes and showering if necessary. Have a stash of clean spare clothing (encourage parents to donate unwanted items).

If you feel the need to label the clothes as belonging to the setting, do so discretely so that the child is not identified as having had to have their clothes changed.

Health and medicines

Policies and guidance for administering medicines are clearly addressed in the statutory framework. Sometimes children require medication for an ongoing condition which means that staff in the setting will need to administer it. Written parental consent is required. As well as the parent's name and signature, this should include:

- the child's name and the name of the medicine

- method of administering, e.g. inhaler, drops etc.

- the precise dosage and timing (with detailed information on the precise circumstances and symptoms for which the medicine might be given)

- inhalers should be readily available at all times, but all other medicines should be kept in a locked cupboard

- each medicine should be clearly labelled with the child's name – always check the name label first before administering

- keep a written record of all medicines given, including child's name, date and time, name of medicine and dosage

- also make a note of any problems administering the medicine to the child which might mean the full dose hasn't been taken, or highlight the need to reassess the way it is given

- make sure that all information is kept up to date and ensure that medicine that is used irregularly (e.g. inhalers) are checked and within the 'use by' date.

(Adapted from Bruce, Meggitt, Grenier 2010).

Something to think about

O Children have a healthy interest in dirt and bodily functions but quickly pick up on adults' judgements and prejudices. How do you ensure that your comments are balanced and non-judgmental? How do you enable children to develop a balanced and rational attitude to their bodies and cleanliness?

O There is ongoing debate about whether soap and water is as good as hand sanitisers. How do you keep up to date with the current and changing issues on this subject with regards to children and how will this affect your practice?

It is also crucial that any staff medications should be securely stored and out of reach of children at all times. This requires that staff have somewhere on site where their bags and belongings can be stored. This is also the case with visitors, who may have medication in bags, pockets etc. It is always advisable to give visitors somewhere to securely store their belongings if they are spending time in the setting around children.

EYFS Unique child Card 1:4 Growing and developing

○ For babies and children rest and sleep are as important as good food.

Sleep and rest, food and nutrition

Sleep and rest

While children are sleeping, their bodies are not just resting, they are also growing and just as importantly their brains are busy processing all the memories and learning from the day that has just passed. 'Between infancy and adulthood, we spend more than one third of our lives asleep, during which the body replenishes its energy and the brain reprocesses experiences stored during the waking hours'. (Karmiloff-Smith 2012).

Studies by University College London, using the Millennium Cohort Study (MCS) have found that irregular bedtimes can lead to hyperactivity and emotional difficulties in young children. This is thought to be because of the impact that irregular bedtimes have on our circadian rhythms, our 'body clocks' that respond to the light and dark of day and night. When these are disrupted it causes a kind of jet lag that can induce disturbed behaviours. The good news is that if regular bedtimes are introduced, then the disturbance is reduced and behaviours improve. (Morton 2013).

Children vary in the amount they need to sleep, but typically a child under 5 will need between 11 to 12 hours sleep with younger children also benefiting from a nap during the day. Babies obviously will sleep more frequently and pre-term babies may sleep for even longer periods.

Recent research suggests that pre-school children might actually learn better after a nap (Williams and Horst 2014), as 'sleep consolidation' has the potential to increase learning and memory. Most early years settings will make provision for babies to sleep and for older children to nap or have a rest time, although increasing pressures to focus on active learning are beginning to affect this. Dr Horst, the co-author of the research states that 'Many preschool children take an afternoon nap, yet classroom naps are increasingly being curtailed and replaced due to curriculum demands. Given the growing body of evidence that sleep consolidation has a significant effect on children's learning, such policies may be doing our children a huge disservice'. (Jones Russell 2014). This is surely something to think carefully about when reviewing sleep and rest policies. Clearly, children do not need to be 'on the go' all the time to be making the most of their learning.

Getting the balance right

Settings also have to balance the needs of parents who don't want their children napping in case it stops them sleeping easily later or how wakeful they are during the night. This is a valid concern, but most settings will have a sleep and rest policy that they share with parents on admission. This will state the importance of responding to the needs of individual children and letting them sleep when they are tired. Key people who are attuned to their children will recognise the signs that a child is getting tired and needs a nap or rest time to be able to function well. Together with the parents, review the situation regularly as the child matures and the need for sleep during the day shifts as the child's energy levels grow. (Mathieson 2014).

Sleep and stress

However, there is no denying that poor sleep can be a major cause of stress in families with young children. As Angela Underdown describes 'undoubtedly there are many factors involved but it may be that stress makes the parent less able to pick up on infant cues and so the infant is less able to regulate sleep patterns, which causes more stress'. (2007). This cycle of stress affects the wellbeing of everyone in the family and parents may look to practitioners for help in establishing good nightime sleeping routines. It is important to be aware that there may be cultural differences in the way that families organise sleeping arrangements and that being judgemental or prescriptive is unlikely to be helpful.

Rest and 'down time'

There are various guidelines for providing sleeping areas for babies and young children, but many settings find that sleep nests or 'coracles' allow children to make independent decisions about times for sleep. A quiet corner with cushions and blankets also offers a place for 'down time' when children just want somewhere to rest quietly. Personal items from home provide comfort and familiarity when children are sleepy and can make a big difference to their wellbeing when they wake up after a nap, not always knowing where they are.

Something to think about

O How do you balance the day so that babies and children have time for rest and relaxation?

O How does your environment support children's individual choices for vigorous activity or rest ? Where can children go independently for naps or quiet times?

O A 'tuned in' carer recognises when their children are tired. What are the signs you recognise in the children in your key group? How are you able to respond to individual needs for rest or activity?

O If you work with babies, do you know how each child likes to be settled and how they usually wake?

Reception classrooms are often busy, lively places with lots going on, but it is worth remembering that some reception children may just have turned four and many will find the day very tiring at first. Quiet, comfy spaces indoors and out are just as important at this age and children often know themselves when they need to spend a bit of 'chill out' time looking through a book or just watching what everyone else is up to.

Food, nutrition and allergies

Food and nutrition plays a large part in children's health and wellbeing and is a constant source of concern among policy makers, striving to improve the health of the population in general. It is a sad fact that whilst there is great abundance and waste in terms of food available, we are once again facing food poverty in the UK, as economic stringency affects vulnerable families' ability to pay for food. At the same time we continue to have ongoing concerns about obesity in young children, the impact of sugar and saturated fats on health as well as increasing levels of diet and life style-related diabetes and heart disease. It seems simple to state that good, healthy, cheaply home grown and prepared food is the answer to the nation's food problems, but it is not always a simple matter to abandon the convenience and tastes that have become a habit over the last few decades, when multinational supermarkets have dominated our food sourcing.

It is essential that practitioners are always aware of children who have allergic reactions to certain foods. For some children these reactions could be life threatening.

Food allergies and food intolerances are not the same. An allergy occurs when the immune system reacts to a food or ingredient that is normally harmless for most people. Even tiny amounts can cause potentially life threatening

reactions. When the response is severe, the whole body can be affected and this is known as anaphylaxis.

Food intolerance, for example intolerance to lactose, isn't triggered by the immune system. It is generally not life threatening but can cause uncomfortable digestive symptoms. Coeliac disease is neither an allergy nor a food intolerance. It is an autoimmune disease which is triggered by the gluten found in wheat, rye and barley which can damage the intestine. It can be diagnosed at any age and is a lifelong illness which is managed through a strict gluten-free diet.

Any food can potentially cause a reaction in individuals but those that most commonly trigger an allergy are eggs, milk, soya, wheat, shellfish and nuts. Some children can even have allergic reactions to fruit and vegetables. Get into the habit of always checking labels as some foods contain hidden ingredients that you may not be aware of.

On admission to the setting, always check for dietary information and work closely with parents to ensure that everyone who needs to know, is up to date with the responses required for a child with food issues. Be sensitive to how the child and parent feel about the situation. Be careful not to single out the child and think carefully about how you can ensure their safety whilst at the same time not making them feel different or 'tiresome' because of their condition.

Positive attitudes

The best place to start a healthy diet is in the early years and the framework for the EYFS provides information about the statutory welfare requirements with regard to food and nutrition. The Avon Longitudinal Study of Parents and Children (ALSPAC) has used their body of evidence to link diet not just to a child's early development but also their later educational attainment. Researchers concluded that 'early eating patterns have implications for educational attainment that appear to persist over time, regardless of subsequent changes in diet'. (Feinstein et al. 2008).

So we have a professional responsibility not just to provide the best in food and nutrition for our children, but also to build the positive attitudes and raised awareness that it will make a difference to their future learning as well as their health and wellbeing. A big task, certainly but the chief way we can do this is to model healthy eating habits and share with children the pleasures of relaxed, sociable mealtimes – which should be a high point in their day. Sadly for some children, mealtimes away from home can be a source of extreme anxiety, or at best, just something to be endured and tolerated as adults bustle about amid a clatter of tins and powerful smells.

Family style eating

Eating family style, with practitioners sat with children at tables where they can begin to serve themselves (with help) builds a sense of independence and confidence around food. It has been shown to reduce over-eating as children learn about portion size, taking just enough to start with and helping themselves to more only if they need it. Children are much better at this than we give them credit for and eating alongside them gives practitioners opportunities to observe children who need more help. Children who are observed taking too much, or wasting food can be helped to understand the need to take 'just enough' and come back for more if it is available. Talking about new and unfamiliar food and encouraging children to try a little, is easier when you are all sitting round enjoying it together.

Eating in mixed age groups also provides children with role models and allows older children the opportunity to help younger children. This works particularly well in Foundation Stage Units where nursery and reception age children are grouped together, and in early years settings that include Y1 children, or small rural schools with fewer children across the primary age group.

If it's not logistically possible to provide nursery meals in a family style, then consider serving the meal as usual, but make salads or 'seconds', for example, available for children to serve themselves.

Thinking about reception children

EYFS children in a nursery setting or Foundation Stage Unit are more likely to experience these kinds of informal approaches to meal times, but many children in reception classes find themselves, age four, eating in large noisy, clamouring dinner halls, that no adult would choose to eat in unless they had to. Some schools allow reception children to use the dinner hall first so that the setting is less overwhelming, but ideally, while children are still in the Early Years Foundation Stage, they should:

- eat in small quiet dining areas, sat with their friends, rather than in large noisy dinner halls away from their familiar environment

- ideally eat from plates and bowls, rather than 'airline/prison' trays with compartments for main meal and pudding, which might not be conducive to a good eating experience.

- be able to help with laying and clearing tables, that are made special at meal times, with table cloths kept for the purpose

- be supported to pour their own drinks and serve some of the food themselves

- eat earlier rather than later

- be allowed to take their time

- not be forced to clean their plate – although an inevitable exercise in times of scarcity, this has been linked to obesity in more recent times, with adults not learning as children how to register their own sensations of fullness and who eat from habit or subconscious guilt feelings

- not be left on their own to finish their meal, nor left waiting too long to leave the table when theyhave finished

- be supported in non-judgemental ways to use utensils and eat in ways that might be unfamiliar to them.

Behaviour at mealtimes

Mealtimes and all the little rituals that go with them, are particularly important ways of building group identity and a sense of belonging. The safe predictability of a pleasurable, nurturing routine can build confidence and self-assurance for most, but be aware of children who are anxious or badly behaved around mealtimes.

Consider the possible triggers:

- the impact of transition – from one activity to another and from one environment to another

- eating and meal times might reinforce sadness at being away from home

- the environment might be suddenly overwhelming – smells, noise etc. and adults are busy with practical things and may be less attentive

- fear of being made to eat unfamiliar or disliked food – this can create long term anxieties and food issues

- poor co-ordination and difficulties using utensils

- difficulties sitting still or too close to others.

It is important that you involve children and talk to them about:

- the ingredients used to make the meal, where they come from and how they are prepared

- their favourite meals and foods they enjoy at home

- the names of fruit and vegetables – and how to say them in children's home languages

- which foods are especially nutritious and which should be taken in moderation – this is a better approach than talking about foods that are 'good' or' bad' for us

- portion size – make the most of opportunities to use mathematical language in a 'real life' situation – how much, a little, not too much, a bit more – as well as opportunities for counting and talking about colour, taste, texture

- ways of using knives and forks for different foods and being non-judgemental about other options, e.g. using fingers, chopsticks etc. Remember that it is not 'babyish' to use your fingers – in many cultures it is an efficient, respectful way of eating

- the conventions of good manners – saying 'please and thank you' and passing dishes rather than reaching across people etc. Be aware that conventions are different across cultures and that some languages do not have words for 'please and thank you'. Levels of politeness and deference are equally important but included and reinforced in different ways – so a child for whom English is not their first language may have learnt different ways of being polite and may not use 'please and thank you' automatically

- take the time to listen to children and don't feel you have to always lead the conversation – make the most of the time to sit down and enjoy your food too!

Grow your own

Think about ways you can involve children in the growing and preparation of food to share at snack and mealtimes. Not everyone has the space or expertise to grow their own vegetable garden, but even a window box can provide herbs or tomatoes in the summer. Find out if there are local growing associations nearby who would be interested in helping you (e.g. www.incredibleediblenetwork.org.uk). As well as benefiting from eating home-grown food, there is increasing evidence that connecting with the earth through gardening and growing things is beneficial for physical and emotional wellbeing.

Children who experience the pleasure of harvesting their own potatoes, or sowing seeds for fragrant herbs are likely to want to continue the experience and build their gardening expertise as they grow older. In times of shortage, children who grow to be adults who are skilful food-growers will have talents that will be much in demand.

Snack times

Some settings stop activities so that all the children can sit and share a snack and a drink together. Other settings prefer to offer a 'rolling' snack time, with a designated snack area where children sit and help themselves, in a café style. There are some advantages to both styles, although a fixed snack time doesn't take into consideration a child's need to 'refuel' on their own timescale and to learn to recognise their own bodily sensations of hunger and thirst.

Sometimes children arrive at the setting without having had an adequate breakfast or lunch and benefit from being able to 'top up' when they arrive so that they are energised and ready to make the most of the session. Breakfast clubs have proved to be enormously beneficial in ensuring children have enough nutrition to begin the day and make the most of their learning experience. Where there is cause for concern about a child's nutritional intake and healthy eating, seek advice from managers and SENCos.

Encourage parents to visit and share lunches and snacks. This not only reassures them their children are eating well, but for some who might feel less confident about cooking or understanding nutrition it can help provide them with new and interesting ways of preparing food at home.

Feeding babies and young children

'Feeding an infant and young child is an active and reciprocal act. For successful feeding the adult and child need to 'tune into' one another's behaviour'. (Underdown 2007).

For this reason it is important that a child is fed by someone they know well – and who knows them well. Not just their likes and dislikes, but how quickly they like to eat, how they show they have had enough or just need a pause, how focused they are on the food, how they cope with getting messy and how much they want to do for themselves. Being able to read the child's signals and interpret their needs can only be done successfully when an adult is tuned into the child and can afford to take the time to understand their cues.

Food and nurture

Even as adults we associate good food and mealtimes as nurturing experiences, and attachment and nurture are important aspects of early feeding. The process, whether by bottle or at the breast, should be one of calm reassurance – a hungry baby has no way of knowing that this intolerable hunger is not going to be permanent. When a familiar figure arrives to provide them with what they need, and holds them close and looks at them lovingly while feeding them, a baby slowly learns over time that they can regulate those intolerable feelings of hunger – because they can trust that they will be fed and that it will be a pleasurable experience.

Children and babies in vulnerable families may have adequate nutrition, but may well miss out on the emotionally nurturing elements of being fed. These children in particular, will need practitioners who can spend time on the small nurturing acts that go with mealtimes – 'here comes the aeroplane to feed you...' as they bring the spoon to the child's mouth and 'yum yum that's lovely in your tummy isn't it...', helping the baby to associate being fed with positive feelings.

Some foster and adoptive parents find that older children who have experienced early emotional neglect, need to regress to a much earlier stage and benefit from being wrapped in a blanket and bottle fed or fed with a spoon, long after they would usually have begun to feed themselves. These children and their families need particular support in settings to build up their positive experiences and to sensitively acknowledge the stage they are at without prejudice or expectation. Meeting the child 'where they at' physically and emotionally is always the best starting point. They can then be gradually and sensitively brought to their chronological age, by filling in the important physical and emotional gaps that will otherwise keep them 'stuck' developmentally, even though they may sometimes appear to be making progress on the surface.

Clean your plate!

Many of us have grown up with the subconscious fear that we are letting somebody down if we don't eat up everything put in front of us. Sadly this could be a big contributor to weight issues both as children and in later life. As Pinki Sahota writes in her article on childhood obesity (*Nursery World* 2014) 'There is clear evidence that young children have the ability to self regulate (control) their intake; they know when they have eaten enough.' And yet we continue to see a 'clean plate' as proof that they have eaten well and sufficiently. Adults also apply all sorts of sanctions and rewards to food. 'Eat up all your peas and then you can have your pudding...' sounds more positive than 'No peas – no pudding...' but is ultimately counter productive in exactly the same way. The pudding is seen as a restricted food item which inevitably becomes much more desirable than any amount of tasty vegetables! Sahota suggests that 'restricting access to foods increases preference for and consumption of those foods when they are no longer restricted'. Many of us have an unhealthy relationship as adults,with chocolate or cream cakes, that would suggest this to be true. Our responsibility as parents, carers and educators is to provide both a nutritionally balanced diet and to role model healthy attitudes to food, which includes trusting children to decide and make choices for themselves from the options we provide.

Something to think about

○ What help do practitioners need to adopt healthy eating styles and be good role models for children and families?

○ What ways can you add 'food and eating' into the curriculum, to raise children's awareness of nutrition and introduce unfamiliar foods?

○ How do you use growing and cooking to sustain positive attitudes to health and nutrition?

○ How do you involve parents in your planning when introducing food and nutrition into the curriculum. How do you ensure foods from different cultures aren't introduced merely as a novelty and not something they might eat regularly?

CASE STUDY: GETTING IT RIGHT FOR RECEPTION

The lunchtime experience for EYFS children in reception classes can be long and full of pitfalls. They have to leave their familiar classroom space to eat in a big dinner hall and then spend the rest of the time out in the big playground with dinner staff who may not know them as well as their key people in the classroom. Although the opportunity to play in a big space can be liberating for some children, it can be anxiety inducing for some and lead to problems for others who struggle with the lack of containment.

In order to address these issues, a primary school considered what changes were possible to adapt the experience for reception children. Although the school couldn't provide them with lunch in their classroom, they felt it was important to ensure that they had their lunch first when the dinner hall would be quiet and less overwhelming. Children were served by dinner staff but were able to help themselves to salad from a low level servery. Prior to starting at the school the children and their parents were invited to come and have a school lunch. This reduced some of the anxieties and gave parents the chance to experience lunch and share any concerns.

Once out in the playground, it was felt that a quiet place was needed, not just for reception children, but for others who might feel overwhelmed in the large space, or needed a quiet place to calm down for a while. 'Base Camp' was created as a supervised 'secure base' that children could come and go from during lunch time. Two members of the school ancillary staff took it in turns to supervise the area, ably assisted by older children acting as Buddies. Base Camp is regularly used by a range of children, with varying needs at lunchtime, and reception age boys who were prone to getting into bother have made good use of it. Staff have noted that they return to their classrooms with fewer issues and children are ready to resume work with enthusiasm.

Ask yourself:
- Do you have children who are disturbed by the lunchtime experience? How do they communicate this? Do you recognise challenging behaviour before, during and after mealtimes as evidence of this?
- What are you able to do now to improve the wellbeing of children during snacks and mealtimes? What can you plan to do in the future when funds etc. allow?
- How often do you review your mealtimes from the perspective of a child of varying ages? How do you involve parents in the mealtime process and gather their perspective?

Checklist

In an environment that promotes healthy physical development and wellbeing you will see children who:

- understand the benefits of physical activity and delight in using their bodies in creative ways for activity and movement indoors and out;

- are encouraged to play games on the floor, using their tummies and on their backs as well as crawling and creeping around the space;

- have opportunities for large vigorous movements outside and in, to develop their proprioception and vestibular senses including stretching, rolling, spinning, climbing, running, skipping etc. on different levels and surfaces;

- are able to develop their fine motor skills with activities that encourage manipulation and finger dexterity, and confidence with various tools, as well as malleables e.g. clay and dough;

- can get involved in 'real work' tasks such as sweeping, lifting, carrying, scrubbing etc. as well as 'messy' jobs and play activities that develop proprioception;

- experience personalised and nurturing care routines leading to the natural and unforced development of independent self care with appropriate attention to hygiene;

- have space and opportunities for relaxation, rest and sleep matched to their developmental needs;

- are kept safe from unnecessary risk and hazards whilst being supported to take mindful risks appropriate to their development, and building an awareness of their own potential to assess and manage risk.

You will see practitioners who:

- are knowledgeable about the physical development of babies and young children, including the role played by early reflexes;

- are encouraged to draw on and develop their own physicality to engage and play with children in a range of physical activity including dance and sport, with enjoyment and enthusiasm;

- comply with all health and safety requirements, as set out in the EYFS framework, understanding their relevance to the health and wellbeing of babies and young children;

- support children's sensory development through careful choice of materials, resources and experiences, taking care to gauge stimulation levels appropriate for individual children;

- monitor children who may have difficulties with sensory integration and other aspects of physical development, seeking advice and guidance as appropriate;

- ensure that policies for physical health and wellbeing are embedded into practice and regularly reviewed;

- know their children well enough to be able to recognise individual signs of ill health and provide comfort and support while children wait to be taken home;

- provide healthy, nutritious food in relaxed, comfortable settings appropriate to children's age and development, ideally in family style groupings, with opportunities to grow, harvest, cook and serve food as appropriate;

- raise parental awareness of the importance of physical development for future learning and wellbeing as well as essential health and safety and risk management;

- are suitably qualified and have access to high quality training and supervision to enable the above.

You will see parents who:

- feel involved in the physical life of the setting in ways appropriate to their capabilities and interests including helping to create and maintain imaginative outdoor spaces, gardening and harvesting, cooking and eating with children;

- are informed about the importance of physical development and the ways that early childhood experiences support their child's future learning and wellbeing;

- feel their contributions and knowledge of their individual children with regard to health and physical development (e.g. feeding, sleeping, milestones etc.) are welcomed and acted upon as appropriate.

Section 3:
Emotional wellbeing

EYFS Unique child Card 1:4

O Babies and children have emotional well-being when their needs are met and their feelings are accepted. They enjoy relationships that are close, warm and supportive.

O Making friends and getting on with others helps children to feel positive about themselves and others.

O Children gain a sense of well-being when they are encouraged to take responsibility and to join in by helping with manageable tasks that interest them.

O Children feel a sense of belonging in the setting when their parents are also involved in it.

Attachment theory and regulation

'The child who really 'matters' to another person, usually the parent, seems to have an invaluable resource for health and well-being'. (Underdown 2007).

The statement above reminds us of the importance of our earliest relationships – and that feeling connected or 'attached' to someone else is fundamental to our emotional health. Attachment theory, first brought to public notice in the 1950s by John Bowlby has long been debated, but more recent neuroscientific developments would seem to confirm that brain development is linked

to our early attachment experiences with caregivers. Although we don't have to be neuroscientists to work with young children, having a good understanding of attachment theory and basic brain development helps us to better understand how emotional wellbeing develops and why it is so important.

Imagine what it might feel like to be floating out in space attached only by a lifeline to your spaceship. How important is that connection to you? The clue is in the word 'lifeline' – not only is your survival dependent upon it, but it also allows you to go out and take the huge risk of floating out in space, marvelling at the view and the experience as well as performing any activities and tasks that you are there to do. Imagine how you would feel if that lifeline were to be cut, leaving you with limited oxygen and no contact with other people who know you are there and can help you? (O'Connor 2012). This is a simplistic analogy but it can help us to understand why attachment is so important to human beings.

Films such as Gravity (2014) play on these fears for dramatic effect. We need the 'lifeline' that attachment provides to prevent us from floating away and being lost, left on our own without the oxygen that we need to survive and the contact with others which is just as important. We need to feel 'attached', so that we feel secure and safe

enough to take risks and go about our everyday lives. For a baby or small child to not feel that they 'matter' to someone is as intolerable as being left to float in space with no air to breathe and no-one to care. (O'Connor 2012).

Emotional regulation

Attachment theory suggests that newborns begin the attachment process instinctively, when they seek to feed. They create an initial primary attachment figure (usually, but not always, the mother) and will look to them to soothe and regulate their 'intolerable' feelings of hunger, fear or discomfort. Each time their need is met, a 'pathway' is created in the brain that becomes stronger and faster with each repetition.

This neural connection, over time, enables them to trust that their need will be met and enables them to begin to cope (when they are a little older) if they have to wait a bit longer for food, to have their nappy changed, or for someone to pick them up. This is called 'emotional regulation' and in the beginning, the child relies on the people closest to them to help them regulate their emotions. With enough good experiences, eventually the neural pathways in the child's brain develop well enough to enable the child to 'self-regulate' – to be able to cope with minor stresses and setbacks without relying on others and 'to manage or regulate their own emotions'. (Underdown 2007).This is an important feature of emotional health and wellbeing, and sadly some children don't have the benefit of enough good experiences, to develop those strong connections in their brain. So they don't learn to trust that they 'matter' enough to someone else and they live with 'intolerable' stress and anxiety, which they may act out in lots of different ways. We will return to this later when we look at the impact of insecure attachment.

Primary and secondary attachment figures

Bowlby described the primary attachment figure as the person the child instinctively turned to when troubled. But no parent is superhuman enough to be there physically and emotionally for a child every minute of the day – and Bowlby was very clear that they don't have to be. Attachment theory suggests that every child also has a 'back-up' team of several secondary attachment figures with whom the child has a strong attachment and will be comfortable with, in the absence of the primary attachment figure. This is likely to include the father or main carer's partner, as well as siblings, grandparents, friends and other relations.

The secondary attachment figures serve a very important purpose in supporting the primary attachment figure, as well as being there for the child. Bowlby was very clear that the task of parenting was a hard one, but he (along with others like Bruno Bettelheim and Donald Winnicott) was also keen to stress that it needed to be 'good enough' rather than perfect. Secure attachment is 'good enough' attachment – where the child has experienced enough positive experiences to have laid down strong pathways in the brain to ultimately enable self-regulation.

Attunement

When there is a 'good enough' connection between the child and their primary and secondary attachment figures then they are able to 'tune into' the very particular needs of that child. Getting to know the distinctive cries of a new baby, or understanding the early babble of a toddler is something that only someone who spends time with that child will be able to do. Although time isn't all that's involved – we've got to care enough to want to engage with their crying and babbling to be able to understand the child. This means being able to set aside our own priorities and to have the 'space' available in our minds to be able to focus on the child. Being able to tune in like this leads to 'attunement', or what Angela Underdown refers to as 'an empathic responsiveness between two individuals, which subtly conveys a shared emotion'. (Underdown 2007).

The impact of insecure attachment on wellbeing

Unfortunately some children don't have enough of these early experiences of attunement. Remind yourself of that astronaut floating about in space with no lifeline, and no sense that they are connected to anyone else in the world. At its most extreme, attachment difficulties can make a child (or adult) subconsciously feel they are completely alone in the world and have only themselves to depend on for survival, even if they are surrounded by family or supportive adults. This makes it difficult (if not impossible) for them to trust anybody (even those people who try to care for them) and to let themselves become attached to anybody. They find it difficult to self-regulate and live with high stress levels as they are always on guard for any threat. Because the required pathways in their brain have not developed, they don't understand the consequences of their actions and they find it hard to empathise with others or to show sympathy or remorse. This is 'disordered' attachment at its most extreme.

As awareness and understanding of the impact of insecure attachment on the brain has grown, researchers and specialists have tried to explain this more in terms of the 'trauma' or 'insult' to the brain that happened when the child didn't receive good enough attachment experiences in their earliest years. Many children who are

'Looked After' or adopted, may have lived with neglect or multiple disruptions to their attachment, and may display emotional or behavioural challenges as a result of the developmental trauma they have experienced. This can make it very difficult for them to accept care and affection from their new caregivers and to learn to trust. It is important to remember that the trauma of their early life does not disappear just because they have been removed to a place of safety and that their 'disability' is often largely invisible as they may present as though they are 'coping' – until their behaviour shows you otherwise.

However, with enough of the right therapeutic interventions, the brain can create new pathways, allowing these children to develop increasingly secure attachments and for them to learn to trust carers enough to allow themselves to be taught, as well as loved and cared for.

Barriers to attachment

Attachment issues are not always extreme, however, and are not limited to children who have experienced severe trauma and disruption. There are a number of factors that can cause attachment difficulties and it is important to recognises that some of these can be outside of the parents' control. These include:

- pre-natal or birth trauma such as premature birth or medical interventions

- extended or repeated separations, e.g. hospitalisation of the mother

- post-natal depression

- child's undiagnosed or unresolved painful illness, e.g. colic, ear infections etc.

- multiple changes in caregiver, for example, foster placements

- parental history of drug/substance abuse

- parents or carers with their own insecure or disordered attachments.

Behaviour as communication

All behaviour is an attempt to communicate something, and an understanding of how insecure attachment affects emotional health and wellbeing can help us to handle those challenging behaviours. Insecure attachment can be seen in two different styles of behaviour – the extent of which depends on the individual child and their responses to external events.

Some children (and adults) can display both kinds of behaviour depending on the circumstances and the degree of stress, or perceived threat, that they are experiencing.

Insecure avoidant attachment

This develops when a child's experiences have led to them not being able to believe that their needs will be met, instead learning to 'fend for themselves' emotionally, if not (or sometimes as well as) physically. They may exhibit a range of behaviours including appearing withdrawn; not looking to others for help or comfort; being unemotional; hating to fail and being difficult to teach, preferring to tackle things themselves, though fear of failure can also lead to them refusing to try.

Insecure ambivalent attachment (sometimes called anxious attachment)

This develops when a child can't be certain that their needs will be met – sometimes parents/carers have been emotionally and physically available, sometimes not. This leads to behaviours that will help reassure the child that they are not forgotten about e.g. being clingy; needing constant reassurance; over emotional and attention seeking often through negative behaviours.

Adults who are really in tune with a child, are able not just to recognise the underlying reasons for the child's attitudes and dispositions, but also learn to spot the triggers that can result in behaviours that might otherwise be dismissed as aggressive, demanding or manipulating. Attuned adults recognise the distress communicated by the behaviours and are able to provide the regulation and containment needed.

Key people and social relationships

Statutory Requirements

3.26 Each child must be assigned a key person. Their role is to help ensure that every child's care is tailored to meet their individual needs (in accordance with paragraph 1.11), to help the child become familiar with the setting, offer a settled relationship for the child and build a relationship with their parents.

Rosemary Roberts highlights 'knowledge' as a defining feature of a key person. Key people 'bring a knowledge of child development [...] together with a detailed knowledge of their individual children'. (Roberts 2010).

The Key Person Approach

This is subtly different to a key worker system which is more about administrative needs and has limitations in its ability to support children's health and wellbeing. The Statutory

Requirement 3:26 suggest the roles expected of a key person, but, in isolation these will have little impact on wellbeing without the supervision and support that key people need to do their job properly. Building a true key person approach is challenging, but brings huge benefits to the child, the family and the practitioners involved. As Jennie Lindon reminds us in her book *The Key Person Approach* 'Young children need, and deserve, the same high quality of nurture and personal attention wherever they spend their days'. (2010).

Ideally, every child needs more than one key person; practitioners are also not superhuman and sometimes get sick, have a day off or work in shift patterns. It is pointless for a child to make a strong relationship with a key person, who is then not available to the child for half the day, or disappears for a week with the flu. Key people can work as a pair, or with a back up team or 'buddy' to ensure the child always has available, someone with whom they feel connected in a special way. Elinor Goldschmied and Sonia Jackson (1994) writing in 'People Under Three: Young Children in Daycare' remind us that when children are first away from home they are the only ones who don't really know why they are there. Away from home, the key people become part of their secondary attachment 'back up' team.

There are a range of ways to organise the key person approach, but a fundamental purpose of having key people should always be to support emotional connection. This is particularly important during transitions when the child can easily feel lost, abandoned and not 'held in mind'.

Feeling 'held in mind' and emotional containment

Feeling 'held in mind' is a fundamental aspect of 'good enough' attachment that not only allows the child to feel safe in the knowledge that they are 'known' and cared about, but also reassures the child that they too can retain a sense of the important people in their lives even when they are not with them. It is also linked to attunement and emotional containment in the way that adults support children, by being 'not always on top of them, but available'. (Manning

Morton 2014). The aim is to provide emotional 'containment' as much as physical help. This is particularly important for children with behavioural issues, for whom the presence of a tuned-in adult somewhere in the room, reading the child's emotional cues (Roberts 2010) helps them stay regulated when things threaten to get too stressful.

How the Key Person approach supports attachment

Bowlby described four defining characteristics of attachment:

● Proximity maintenance – wanting to stay close to the people to whom we are attached

● Safe haven – returning to our attachment figures when we are frightened or distressed

● Separation distress – feeling anxious when our attachment figures are not there

● Secure base – our attachment figures provide a secure base from which we can go out and explore the world.

In this model, feeling distress at being separated is to be expected as it indicates attachment. We continue to feel distress even as adults, when we are separated from people to whom we are attached. However, while we as adults can (generally) rationalise our feelings, and know that we can survive distressing feelings, children can't. This is why we need to create a strong key person approach that provides the child with secondary attachment figures or 'important people' (Roberts 2010) who will help them through difficult times and why we must acknowledge and honour children's feelings when they are sad (or angry) at being separated from a parent as they transition into the setting or to school.

Although the key people will never (and should never attempt to) take the place of the child's primary attachments with their family, they will probably over time, provide all the defining features of attachment as described above.

Secure base

In particular, the child's key people will become the 'secure base' that provides the sense of safety that allows the child to explore and to take, as Bowlby described it, little 'excursions' out into the world. He felt that this was important even as we grow into adulthood. 'All of us, from the cradle to the grave, are happiest when life is organised as a series of excursions, long or short, from the secure base provided by our attachment figure(s)'. (Bowlby 1988).

This is not only important for a child's emotional wellbeing, it is also fundamental to the way that learning can take place when a child feels safe enough to explore and take risks. Children who aren't anxious or fearful and are 'high on emotional well-being have 'space' in their minds to take on new ideas' (Underwood 2007) allowing them to have higher levels of engagement with life and learning. Rosemary Roberts also considers the key person to play a very important role as 'companion' or playmate – just as the child's primary carers and extended family have done at home. (Roberts 2010). Jools Page reminds us of the importance of warmth in the relationship between a child and their key people when she writes about the need to consider a place for 'professional love' in the practitioner role and the challenges it presents to get the balance right. (Page, Clare and Nutbrown 2013).

'Triangle of trust' – children, parents and key people

The key person approach can also provide security and emotional containment for parents. They need to feel that the practitioners looking after their children are not only tuned in to their children, but are also tuned into them, how they feel about being apart from their children and the experiences they want for them. Elfer, Goldschmied and Selleck describe the special relationship between parents and key people as a 'triangle of trust'. (Elfer et al. 2012). This trusting relationship ensures the wellbeing of children. It is supported by the warm, respectful and friendly relationships practitioners have with parents and families, particularly during initial transitions from home to the setting and the daily transitions at the beginning and end of every session.

Importance of supervision for key people

If, as many people believe, the quality of the key person relationship can have the biggest impact on the wellbeing of children attending early years settings, then we need to also consider the wellbeing of the key people. Elfer, Goldschmied, and Selleck are clear that for the key person approach to be successful, then supervision (in the therapeutic sense) must be provided. This means that key people receive regular private, discussion time with a mentor or manager to talk about all the aspects of their job – the good, the bad and even the ugly, which is why these discussions should not be linked in any way to performance management. They should provide opportunities for practitioners to 'offload' to a colleague they can trust, all the emotional challenges of working in such a close relationship with children and their families and access support and guidance if needed.

This does much to ensure the health and wellbeing of individual practitioners and ensures that the key person approach is managed effectively. In an ideal world,

---

Something to think about

○ Think about the ways children experience the warmth of your relationship with their parents.

○ How do you handle conflicts with parents so that children's wellbeing is not affected?

Something to think about

○ What do you need in your working role to ensure your emotional wellbeing?

○ How do you ensure that your training and supervision needs are communicated to managers?

---

opportunities for training and supervision should be available for all practitioners working with young children and their families, particularly those providing family support and outreach work. Supervision of this kind is the equivalent of the oxygen mask that drops down in an aeroplane in an emergency. Adults who don't put their own mask on first may quickly become unable to help the children who rely on them. Staff wellbeing is an important feature of children's wellbeing. Tired, anxious, frustrated or unhealthy adults are unlikely to be able to provide the best support for children's wellbeing.

Belonging

A sense of belonging – to a family, a setting, a community, is a very important part of wellbeing. Wearing the same uniform or carrying the same book bag do not in themselves engender a sense of belonging. The way a child and their family feel welcomed, eagerly awaited, involved and respected contribute to a real sense of belonging – and to feeling like 'a fish in water'.

We talk about feeling like 'a fish out of water' when we mean we don't feel right, we don't belong or aren't suited to the place we find ourselves in. Taken literally, a fish out of water is in the wrong place and will soon die. A fish in water can take for granted that it's in the right environment and is able to get on and do what it does best. Ferre Laevers uses the phrase to describe children who feel 'alright' (Ferre Laevers 2005) and who have high levels of wellbeing and involvement.

Children who feel at home in the setting, who are relaxed and sure of themselves have more space in their heads for learning and developing. They are comfortable with the routines and know the limits and boundaries of what

Something to think about

○ How do you help parents feel they are welcomed into your setting?

○ How do you know when a parent feels welcomed?

○ How do you know when a child feels they belong?

○ What barriers might there be for some children and their families? How do you address these, so that everyone feels they belong in the setting, in their own way?

is considered acceptable behaviour in the setting. Te Whāriki, the New Zealand curriculum guidance for Early years points out that, 'The early childhood education setting should be like a caring home: a secure and safe place where each member is entitled to respect and to the best of care. The feeling of belonging, in the widest sense, contributes to inner well-being, security, and identity'. (Te Whāriki – Part C Strand 2).

In order to feel you really belong somewhere, you need to feel that you have something to contribute to the group and that your contributions are both invited and accepted. A sense of belonging can be even more crucial to the child with a disability or special educational needs – and to their family. A parent needs to feel that their child is accepted for who they are and their contributions to the life of the setting acknowledged, along with their difficulties.

Making friends

Strongly linked to this sense of belonging is the importance of friendship, social interactions and companionship.

'Above everything else, a child needs warm human relationships, and spontaneous feelings of friendship'. (Isaacs 1954 cited in Roberts 2012). Friends are an

important part of a child's life and when children are asked what contributes most to their wellbeing, friendships are always very high up on the list. Having friendships with people beyond their families builds children's emotional literacy. Friendships help them to learn more about themselves, as well as learning more about how other people tick. (Manning Morton 2014).

If friendship is linked to wellbeing, then not having friends, or conflicts with them, can also be linked to a lack of wellbeing. Young children need help from adults or older children to understand about fairness and to mediate conflicts so that friendships can flourish and sustain wellbeing, rather than be the cause of stress and anxiety. Being a 'playmate' and joining in with children's play also allows the adult to foster inclusion and to support children who need help with friendship.

Communication is a key factor in friendship and socialisation, which is why it is so important to make sure that children who speak English as an additional language are well supported. Ideally they need to have, where possible, the chance to make friends with children (and adults) who speak their own home language, as well as being encouraged and supported to make new friendships with children who speak English, and with those with other first languages.

Identity and wellbeing

'If we are to promote children's wellbeing, support healthy development and provide appropriate services for children, we need to gain insight into who they are and who they might become'. (Collins and Foley 2008).

Life stories

No matter how young children might be when we first meet them in a setting, they already come with a 'life story' that

Something to think about

○ Did friends make a difference to your wellbeing as a young child? What support did you have / would have liked to develop and sustain friendships at a young age?

○ How do you monitor children's friendships and use the information to:
   a) assess and maintain wellbeing
   b) build social skills
   c) support your planning for groups of children?

started long before they were born, based on aspects of their family and community identity. This includes beliefs and attitudes as well as ethnicity and language etc. They will also have a gender identity, which generally comes not just from the sex they were born into but, in the first instance, also from the gender expectations of their family and wider community, though this may change.

Our identity has strong links with our wellbeing, self image and self esteem, but is about so much more than just 'where' we were born and to 'whom'. The more a child is aware of themselves and has a strong sense of identity, the more capacity they have ultimately to become aware of other people, to be curious about them and the way their minds work. Without a strong self awareness of our own, it is harder to understand why people do the things they do and, just as importantly, to be able to predict what they might do.

Identity changes over time, as a result of both the choices we make as individuals and the events that happen to us – and the ways in which we respond to them. Fundamental to our work in the early years is an appreciation of the 'whole' child and all the many facets of their identity, starting with who they are now, but with no limits on who they may become.

Getting to know you

Home visits help give a rounded picture of the whole child in different contexts and are very important in supporting the transition process. A shy child at nursery might feel able to display a very different side of themselves on their home territory and all children benefit from the sense of familiarity that comes with meeting their key people for the first time, in their own home. How lovely is it to see a child glowing with pride and recognition when they can say *'You came round my house!'*

Home visits may be costly in time and people, but done well, they make such a difference to early relationships between

children, key people and their parents. Always take two people as this is not only important for safeguarding, it also allows one person to focus on the child while the other gathers essential information from the parent and provides them with the opportunity to share concerns etc. Pay special attention to getting names right as these are fundamental to a child's sense of identity, as well as finding out about likes and dislikes, interests and motivations and any health issues. Talk to parents about how you monitor children's wellbeing and why you value it. Most parents will express the need for their child to be 'happy' when they are away from them. They need to know that we will be able to recognise the small indicators particular to their child's wellbeing – and that we are willing to learn how best to respond to them when they are tired, unwell, anxious or out of sorts.

What's the difference?

There is a stage in early childhood development when children begin to register gender and to work out which 'club' they belong to. Sometimes this involves displaying overt 'girlness' or' boyness' in ways that our society generally recognises, and advertising and toy companies capitalise upon. Pink Princesses and Blue Pirates sadly seems to sum this up currently, though the fashion may change in future years.

Exploring these aspects of being a girl or a boy are not unhealthy in themselves. The danger lies in a childhood that offers only these options and denies children the myriad of different ways in which they can be 'who they are' – some of which may involve being part of a 'gender' club. It is just as important for both boys and girls that they know and value their gender identity, whatever it may be, but are confident that it is only part of who they are and not something that limits them.

This is true of all other 'labels' that may become part of a child's identity, particularly with regard to health, special educational needs and disability. Labels have their uses, particularly when they raise awareness and understanding of the challenges faced by a child with additional needs (and their family). Labels can also help to ensure they receive the resources required to be able to thrive as well as any other child.

Something to think about

○ Pink for girls and blue for boys? Do your colleagues all share the same opinions about gender?

○ How do you explore equalities and inclusion issues as a team and support parents to understand your policies?

CASE STUDY: FEELING AT HOME

A foundation stage unit of an inner city primary school was used to having visits from practitioners from around the country and across the globe.

More unusually, they were hosts to an official from an educational NGO (Non-Government Organisation) in Bangladesh who was researching British early years care and education, prior to adding nursery classes to their provision. He worked with the team for a fortnight and was surprised to find himself mopping floors and mixing paints as much as he was involved with direct teaching.

He set to, though, and contributed well to the life of the unit, where nursery and reception children were fully integrated and spent a lot of time outdoors in the early years garden. He commented positively on how he was made to feel welcome and how he noticed this was the same for children and their families.

On his final day, as he was helping tidy up, he reflected that the aspect that seemed to underpin all the work of the unit was that it 'felt more like a second home than school' and that he could see how this had such a positive impact, not just on children's wellbeing, but also their development and learning. He described some of the physical features he thought contributed to this but added that as the children all came from such varying home backgrounds it must be the attitudes and dispositions of the early years team that contributed most to this sense of being at home in the unit.

Ask yourself:
- What are the features of provision that contribute to helping a child feel at home in your setting?
- How do you help all children feel at home in a very diverse setting?
- Do you feel at home in your setting?
- How do you support new colleagues to feel they belong?

Labels are not damaging in themselves, or indeed negative, but people sometimes shy away from them because of the fear that they will be used to oppress or discriminate against and that the label will lead to biased opinions. But we need to remember that the child is always much more than their 'label' – and that it is our professional responsibility to avoid lazy stereotypes influencing our practice.

Bias and anti-bias

Statutory Requirements

3.66 Providers must have and implement a policy, and procedures, to promote equality of opportunity for children in their care, including support for children with special educational needs or disabilities. The policy should cover: how the individual needs of all children will be met (including how children who are disabled or have special educational needs, will be included, valued and supported, and how reasonable adjustments will be made for them); the name of the Special Educational Needs Co-ordinator (in group provision); arrangements for reviewing, monitoring and evaluating the effectiveness of inclusive practices that promote and value diversity and difference; how inappropriate attitudes and practices will be challenged; and how the provision will encourage children to value and respect others.

Bias is an inclination, an attitude, a belief or prejudice, for or against someone (or a group of people) that could result in unfair treatment. Anti-bias presents an active challenge to bias and any negative stereotypes, or associated prejudices or discrimination. It challenges issues in society like sexism and racism, not by denying our differences, but by embracing them in a way that allows us to acknowledge just how prejudice and bias affects the wellbeing of everyone.

Bias happens all the time and not just to 'other people', though we don't all experience it in the same way. Sometimes bias can support our identity or sometimes it will attack it. Children whose identity is not well supported are likely to experience 'internalised oppression'. This can occur in relation to race and ethnicity, faith and belief, gender, ability, language and culture as well as socio-economic group and appearance. Remember how it felt to be the only child in the group wearing glasses or the wrong trainers? These intense feelings of being different or not belonging can have a big impact on a child's wellbeing, even at a very early age. If internalised oppression is related to bias with regard to skin colour, language or religion, for example, then wellbeing can be very seriously damaged, possibly for life.

When bias supports our identity, it can lead to a sense of 'internalised superiority'. This sounds ok, but 'superiority' has to imply that someone else must be inferior. Ideally, we want the wellbeing of all our children not to rest on feeling better or more superior than somebody else. (O'Connor A. 2009).

Ellen Wolpert (2005) set out 4 goals of an antibias approach, aiming for each child to gain:

- A confident identity as an individual and as a member of multiple cultural groups (e.g. gender, race, ethnicity, class etc.)

- Comfortable empathic interaction with people from diverse backgrounds

- The ability to recognise bias and injustice

- The ability to stand up, individually and with others, against bias or injustice.

These goals go hand in hand with self regulation, resilience and empathy as life skills that contribute not just to individual wellbeing but also to the collective wellbeing of society. With these skills you are likely to neither be a bully or to allow yourself to be bullied.

Empathy and resilience

Maia Szalavitz and Bruce Perry in their book 'Born to Love' describe empathy as 'The ability to stand in another's shoes and to care about what it feels like to be there'. This is not something children can do by themselves to begin with, but programmes such as 'Roots of Empathy' and the Persona Dolls approach enable us to support children with the process at an early age. But first a child must have experienced empathy, in order to be able to feel it for someone else. This is linked to the self-awareness that comes from the positive feedback and emotional regulation provided by parents and familiar carers in a child's early life. (Robinson 2010). When we talk to babies about feelings, we are helping them identify their feelings and emotions. These 'mind related' comments at an early age can make a big difference to a child's ability, not only to understand their own feelings but to be aware of them in others. (Meins et al. 2002). Being able to see something from another's perspective – or having a 'theory of mind', typically develops around the age of four or five years, although it is possible that it might develop earlier in children who are exposed to lots of 'mind-related' talk at an early age as well as lots of stories and pretend play.

Self awareness also plays a part in the development of resilience. It is easy to think that resilience develops as a result of challenges and difficulty. 'What doesn't kill you only makes you stronger', is how the saying goes, but for once the old wives might not be strictly accurate. Too much difficulty, trauma, disruption and insufficient love and care at an early age sometimes end up as a newspaper headline recounting the sad death of a child at the hands of an abusive or neglectful family. But there are many more children who are technically 'saved' from abuse or danger who don't grow up to be resilient, healthy individuals. Their lives, sadly are more likely to be marked by further difficulty, as they struggle with physical and mental health issues directly related to their early trauma. These children, despite being placed with loving foster carers or adoptive parents, have an increased likelihood of addiction and substance abuse, of school exclusion and learning difficulties and of poor life chances, sometimes leading to prison, ill health, suicide or early death. These examples are at the extreme end of the spectrum. However, if they suggest that too much hardship and difficulty do not make children 'healthily resilient', then perhaps having enough 'good enough' experiences in early life is a factor for more resilience to hardship and challenge later on?

There is no denying that some people seem to have a greater disposition for resilience, and that a degree of measured challenge is important in strengthening children's disposition for perseverance and problem solving. But by putting children's wellbeing at the heart of our practice in early care and education, we are helping to build a healthy resilience in children who will surely need it in the uncertain times to come.

Safe enough to make mistakes

As a society currently driven by testing and targets, we are also in danger of instilling in our children the fear that making mistakes and getting things wrong is too big a risk to take. We all know we learn by our mistakes and though we constantly tell children this, we don't always reinforce it by our actions if we present children with fixed learning objectives all the time, rather than allow for 'possible learning outcomes' that can't always be planned for at the start of every session. Open-ended questions and activities without fixed outcomes encourage children to follow their own line of enquiry. They also reassure them that there isn't always a right answer that they have to hunt for, (or work out what was in an adult's mind) just to win praise or pass a test. Freedom to make mistakes, to start all over again – or to adapt our errors and make something useful out of them – is essential to creativity. Authors, artists and inventors take risks when they explore new ideas, as do scientists and physicists, who try out new theories without knowing first whether or not they will work. A degree of resilience, both physical and emotional, enables all of us to take mindful and creative risks that can bring about positive outcomes for wider society as well as ourselves.

Play and tasks

The importance of play

'We can always rely on children for the motivation and means to play, but they need to be able to rely on adults to protect and provide time and space for play'. (Springate and Foley 2008).

Children will play anywhere, with pretty much anything and

generally with enthusiasm. Sometimes there is shouting and shrieking as they run around exuberantly, other times there is quiet concentration as they build with blocks or create a story with toy cars or little animals. They play together and they play alone, or with imaginary friends. Play is fun – and it's also serious business.

It contributes to children's wellbeing in a variety of ways. It allows children the chance to 'act out' their experiences, particularly their observations of adults, and enables them to 'rehearse' life skills. It can also be therapeutic, allowing experiences that trouble or worry them to be played out in a safe space. It can take learning forward as a child explores a new experience, achieves a new skill or extends their abilities. Sometimes play revisits and consolidates old experiences, providing opportunities to explore schema and do something over and over again. It is very beneficial when it is self-initiated, although children love to respond to a trigger or stimulus from an adult or another child, from an interesting event or situation or an inspiring 'thing' to play with. They also benefit from adults who offer 'companiable attention, (Roberts 2010) and who can meet children in what Vygotsky called the 'zone of proximal development' where they support and extend the play, by tuning into what the child would like to be able to do but can't yet and by giving them help to be able to do it. Free-flow play as described by Tina Bruce (1991) suggests that some play experiences draw children into a state of flow, also described by Mihaly Csikszentmihalyi (1990) as a condition of intense personal satisfaction that comes from the exploratory urge inherent in some kinds of play. So we know a lot of learning takes place during play, but just as importantly, that play has value in itself. We have a professional responsibility, therefore, to provide the time and space, particularly indoors and out, that children need for periods of uninterrupted, sustained play.

Real life tasks

When children imitate or join in with adults in real life tasks, they are not only using purposeful activity to rehearse life skills, they are also engaging in activities that promote their physical development and a sense of agency.

Examples of real life tasks include:

- planting and caring for plants and harvesting

- preparing, cooking and serving food

- laying and clearing tables and washing up

- cleaning surfaces, washing dolls clothes

- sorting, tidying and sweeping

- lifting and carrying.

Exposure to 'green spaces' and working with soil, plants and the natural world outdoors, in particular, improves physical and psychological health as there is now evidence to suggest our immune systems need input from the biodiversity of the natural environment. (Rook 2013).

Lifting, carrying and sweeping are examples of real life tasks that are important in proprioceptive development, as they involve using the muscles and joints and working at the body's limits.

When a young child picks up a pen and writes a 'shopping list' for the first time, they are 'a writer', and the same is true of lots of activities that allow them to behave 'as if' they were a reader, or a mathematician or a scientist, in the same way that they pretend to be a daddy or a train driver or a shopkeeper. When this kind of 'real life' activity is self initiated by the child, (rather than directed by an adult) it is not only playful, but it also feels good and acts as a powerful motivator to explore more opportunities to extend and improve their physical mastery in developmentally appropriate ways. Self directed achievements such as these, often lead to a sense of being 'chuffed' with oneself, prompting early years specialists to add 'chuffedness' to the list of indicators of wellbeing. (Huleatt 2014).

Checklist

In an environment that promotes wellbeing you will see children who are:

- relaxed;

- self-confident;

- assertive;

- caring;

- enthusiastic;

- curious;

- comfortable;

- playful;

- adaptable;

- 'chuffed' with themselves, their achievements and those of their friends';

- building attachments with key people and other children;

- growing in self-regulation;

- feeling 'held in mind' by their important people when they are away from them;

- helped to 'hold in mind' those who are important to them;

- feel loved and a sense of 'unconditional regard';

- building resilience;

- developing empathy with others;

- interested in their self identity and what makes them who they are;

- interested in other people, places, activities, events and objects in the natural and manufactured world;

- comfortable with languages and cultural experiences different to their own;

- engaging in sustained, uninterrupted periods of play that promote flow and concentration and allow them to persevere to their own conclusion;

- individually supported through change and transitions by people who know them and understand their physical, social and emotional needs;

- feel like 'fish in water' in the setting.

You will see practitioners who are:

- relaxed

- self-confident

- assertive

- caring

- enthusiastic

- curious

- comfortable

- playful

- adaptable

- resilient

- 'chuffed' with themselves, the children and families they work with and their achievements and progress

- knowledgeable about attachment theory and early brain development and appreciate their importance in emotional health and wealth being

- understand their role as key people, with a focus on building relationship, tuning into the children in their care and holding them in 'unconditional regard'

- comfortable with expressing warmth, affection and 'professional love' in the context of the setting

- well supported by managers and other staff, through training and supervision, allowing them to manage the particular responsibilities of the role

- understand the impact of change on babies and young children and how best to support them through transitions

- feel like 'fish in water' in the setting.

Checklist continued

You will see parents and families who are:

- relaxed;

- self-confident;

- assertive;

- caring;

- enthusiastic;

- curious;

- comfortable;

- playful;

- adaptable;

- resilient;

- 'chuffed' with themselves and their children, their achievements and progress, and that of other children;

- welcomed and valued as their child's first educator and partner in the key person approach;

- well-informed about their child's health and wellbeing;

- able to offer information, ask questions or raise concerns without fear of prejudice;

- supported, where appropriate, with their own health and wellbeing needs;

- feel like 'fish in water' in the setting.

Using story books to promote health and wellbeing

Stories and storytelling are powerful ways to help children explore health and wellbeing. Some storybooks provide explicit information about, for example, eating healthily or naming emotions. Many others will provide implicit support for children in the way that they explore key issues and honour feelings and emotions by portraying characters going though situations that children can relate to, either in the every-day or in the fantasy world. Some stories and books, particularly those based on authentic fairy stories, will explore children's deepest and perhaps unnameable thoughts and fears, ultimately providing wellbeing through deep level identification and satisfying (if not always happy) endings. Repetition of these tales, whether told orally or through books, plays, puppets and props, helps build a repertoire of stories that promote and foster a child's understanding of a long list of essentials such as identity, belonging, family life, challenge, resilience, love and loss.

Books exploring identity

- *What I Like about Me!* (2009) by Allia Zobel Nolan (Reader's Digest Children's Book)
- *I Like Myself!* (2010) by Karen Beaumont, David Catrow (Houghton Mifflin Harcourt)
- *Not All Princesses Dress in Pink* (2010) by Jane Yolen, Heidi E Y Stemple, Anne-Sophie Lanquetin (Simon and Schuster Children Books)
- *Dangerously Ever After* (2012) by Dashka Slater, Valeria Docampo (Dial Books)
- *It's Okay To Be Different* (2009) by Todd Parr (Little, Brown Young Readers)
- *Only One You* (2013) by Linda Kranzde (Taylor Trade Publishing)
- *Elmer* (2007) by David McKee (Andersen)

Books exploring self-help skills

- *How Do I Put it on?* (1993) Shigeo Watanabe, Yasuo Ohtomo (Red Fox)
- *Wonderwise: Wash, Scrub, Brush: A book about keeping clean* (2005) by Mick Manning Brita Granstrom (Franklin Watts)

Books exploring bereavement and loss

- *Are You Sad, Little Bear?: A Book About Learning To Say Goodbye* (2013) by Rachel Rivett, Tina Macnaughton (Franklin Watts)
- *The Goodbye Boat* (2005) by Mary Joslin, Claire St.Louis Little, Claire Warren (Lion Children's Books)

Books exploring family life

- *My Family: Love and Care, Give and Share* (2002) by Lisa Bullard

- *The Family Book* (2010) by Todd Parr
- *All about Me!: A Baby's Guide to Babies* (2008) by David Salariya
- *What's Inside Your Tummy, Mummy?* (2007) by Abby Cocovini

Books exploring mistakes and taking risks

- *Beautiful OOPS* (2010) by Barney Salzberg
- *The Girl Who Never Made Mistakes* (2012) by Mark Pett, Gary Rubinstein

Books exploring emotions and emotional wellbeing

- *The Feelings Book* (2009) by Todd Parr (Little, Brown Young Readers)
- *My Many Coloured Days* (2001) by Seuss (Red Fox)
- *The Way I Feel* (2000) by Janan Cain (Gazelle Book Services)
- *I Love You, Stinky Face* (2003) by Lisa McCourt (Scholastic)

Bringing it all together

'Wellbeing is not about just being okay, coping or surviving. Wellbeing is about thriving, blossoming and flourishing'. (Manning Morton 2014).

Children thrive when their physical and emotional needs are met and understood by special adults who are consistently available to them, who are able to prioritise the child's needs and form loving relationships with them. These special relationships allow the child to grow physically, emotionally, socially and intellectually as they support the child through experiences that stimulate and shape the child's developing brain, and provide the loving containment and regulation required to build the independence and resilience that supports the child to go out and explore their world, with consideration for themselves and others. These special adults, have the knowledge and training to recognise when a child's needs are not being met and when circumstances challenge their wellbeing. They, in turn, are best able to do this when their own wellbeing is assured and safeguarded by supportive work practices, particularly when external factors in the child's life create a serious threat to their health and wellbeing.

Children blossom when they feel listened to, and when their sense of themselves is positively affirmed by others. They know their contributions are welcomed and treated with respect and are encouraged to develop interests and motivations that delight and enthuse them, building and shaping their brain ready to make connections with previous knowledge and to absorb new information and experiences. Their creativity is warmly encouraged in ways that allow them to explore processes as much as outcomes, fostering dispositions of curiosity and reflection that enable them to keep an open mind and pursue activities to a personal conclusion.

Children flourish when they feel safe enough to take risks and to accept challenges – of a physical nature as well as socially, emotionally and intellectually, and relative to their developmental stage. They enjoy communicating with others and use all their senses to fully experience life and to organise their brain to function at its best. They feel a sense of unconditional regard, knowing they are loved and are loveable, and accepted for who they are – on good days and on bad – and are 'held in mind' by their special people even when they are away from them, Thriving, blossoming and flourishing are not steps on the way to health and wellbeing, with one happening first followed by the others. Not only are they all interdependent, they are all relevant to all the different stages of life, from the youngest of babies to the oldest grown-up and to a wide range of living circumstances. Wellbeing shouldn't be something to strive for or grow into – we want children to thrive, blossom and flourish now at whatever age or stage they are at. And we also want all the above criteria for ourselves, now, and long into the future too.

We are not in globally flourishing times however, so there is an even greater urgency that we should be paying attention to children's wellbeing now, so that they have the resilience, not just to withstand their own challenges, but to be able to provide the solutions we are surely going to need in the future.

A crucial part of all that lies in the opportunities we provide for play. Real play that isn't fitted in after the 'proper' work of literacy and maths is done.

Real play that isn't a reward for good behaviour, to be neatly boxed into a 'golden time' or even worse, taken away because of bad behaviour or unfinished work.

Real play that is robust and physical, is sometimes risky and enables children to follow their biological drive for movement, allowing them space for creativity and for exuberance.

Real play that happens in dens and hidey holes (sometimes where adults can't go) – is imaginative and elusive, where the everyday mixes with the magical.

Real play that starts with the child – and even if it has to be interrupted by important things like eating and sleeping – can still be sustained and pursued to a personal conclusion, because it is respected by the adults who are important to that child.

We know that children learn through play and that they play to learn, although we are in danger of giving this lipservice if our understanding of play is limited to topics and themes and activities. But play is also linked to our sense of self and to our emotional health. Children learn to self regulate through their play, to take risks and develop perseverance.

However, as practitioners we also need to be aware of when to step in, not just to support or move the play forward, but also to monitor the wellbeing of **all** children involved. Some play experiences may be less than happy for some children, and it is through sensitive and empathic interventions that we ensure play experiences are fair for all. We are reminded by Deborah Albon writing in *Exploring Wellbeing in the Early Years* (ed Manning Morton 2014)

that although we should 'treasure play and playfulness', there is still a need for practitioners to 'acknowledge a less romantic reality of play: the unfairness and inequity it may engender. This suggests the need for a reflective, critical (but also playful!) approach to play from practitioners in early childhood settings'. (Albon 2014).

Being reflective and critical, (in the sense that we analyse closely, rather than just negatively) are useful terms to describe the work of early years practitioners in general. As we make sense of whatever changes in policy and guidelines might come next in the field of early years care and education, we need to critically analyse the rhetoric, whilst we reflect on what really makes a difference for children's health and wellbeing.

We must remember too that we have the right – as well as the responsibility – to ensure that we play with children, as well as watch them playing. Our ability to be a playful companion is just as important in children's wellbeing and development as any other aspect of our role, during this fundamentally important stage of their lives.

References

Ayres, A.J. (1980/2005) *Sensory Integration and the Child 1980* (Western Psychological Services USA)

Bradford, H. (2012) *The Wellbeing of Children under Three* (Routledge)

Bowlby, J. (2005) *A Secure Base* (Routledge Classics)

Bruce, T. (1991) *Time to Play in Early Childhood Education* (Hodder Education)

Bruce, Meggit, Grenier (2010) *Child Care and Education* (Hodder Arnold)

Bion, W. (1962) *Learning from Experience* (Heinemann)

Bloomfield, S. In a lather (*Nursery World* Feb 2014)

Collins, J., Foley, P. (eds) (2008) *Promoting Children's Wellbeing: policy and practice* (The Policy Press with The Open University)

Csikszentmihalyi, M. (2008) *Flow: The Psychology of Optimal Experience* (Harper Perennial)

Daly, A., O'Connor, A. Physical Development Series (*Nursery World* 2009)

Derman-Sparks, L. (1989) *Anti-Bias Curriculum: Tools for Empowering Young Children* (NAEYC)

Development Matters in the Early Years Foundation stage (available at www.foundationyears.org.uk)

Elfer, Goldschmied, Selleck (2012) *Key Persons in the Early Years* (Routledge)

Feinstein et al. (2008) *Dietary patterns related to attainment in school: the importance of early eating patterns* (Epidemiol Community Health)

Foley, P., Springate, D. (2008) Play Matters (in *Promoting Children's Wellbeing: policy and practice*) Collins and Foley (The Policy Press in association with The Open University)

Gerhardt, S. (2004) *Why love Matters: How Affection Shapes a Baby's Brain* (Routledge)

Goddard Blythe, S. *Perspectives on Early Years Education* (available at www.sallygoddardblythe.co.uk)

Goddard Blythe, S. (2005) *The Well-Balanced Child* (Hawthorn Press)

Goddard Blythe, S. (2009) *Attention, Balance and Coordination: The ABC of Learning Success* (John Wiley and sons)

Goldschmied, E., Jackson, S. (1994) *People Under Three: Young Children in Daycare* (Routledge)

Greenland, P. (2000) *Hopping Home Backwards: Body Intelligence and Movement Play* (Jabadao)

Hirst, K. Nutbrown, C. (2005) *Perspectives on Early Childhood Education: Contemporary Research* (Trentham)

Huleatt, M. *How do you measure chuffedness?* (available at www.communityplaythings.co.uk)

Isaacs, S. (1954) *The Educational Value of the Nursery School* (BAECE)

Jabadao (2009) *More of Me* (online) (available at www.jabadao.org.uk)

Lane, J. (2008) *Young Children and Racial Justice* (National Children's Bureau)

Jones Russell, M. (2014) *An Afternoon Nap Can Help Children Learn New Words* (online) (available at www.nurseryworld.co.uk)

Laevers, F. *Deep-level-learning and the Experiential Approach in Early Childcare and Education* (online) (available at www.cego.be)

Laevers, F. (2005) Well-being and Involvement in Care Settings (online) (available at www.kindengezin.be)

Le Voguer &, Pasch (2014) Physical Well-being: Autonomy, Exploration and Risk-taking (in *Exploring Well-being in the Early Years*) ed. Manning Morton, J. (Open University Press)

Manning Morton, J. ed. (2014) *Exploring Well-being in the Early Years* (Open University Press)

Mathieson, K. (2014) Off to Sleep (*Nursery World* January 2014)

Moran, P. *Neglect: Research Evidence to Inform Practice* (online) (available at www.actionforchildren.org.uk)

Meins et al. (2003) Maternal mind-mindedness and attachment security as predictors of theory of mind understanding (*Child Development* 73)

Morton, K. (2013) Irregular bedtimes for children can cause hyperactive behaviour (*Nursery World* October 2013)

Moylett & Stewart (2012) *Understanding the Revised Early Years Foundation Stage* (Early Education)

Oates, J. Karmiloff Smith, A. Johnson, M.J. (eds) (2012) *Developing Brains* (Open University)

O'Connor, A. Equality and Diversity Series (*Nursery World* 2009)

O'Connor, A. All About ... Neglect (*Nursery World* November 2010)

O'Connor, A. (2012) *Understanding Transitions: Supporting change through attachment and resilience* (David Fulton)

Page, J. Clare, A. Nutbrown, C. (2013) *Working with Babies and Young Children: From Birth to Three* (Sage)

Roberts, R. (2010) *Wellbeing from Birth* (Sage)

Robinson, M. (2007) *Child Development from Birth to Eight: A Journey through the Early Years* (Open University Press)

Robinson, M. (2014) *The Feeling Child: laying the foundations of confidence and resilience* (Routledge 2014)

Read, V. (2009) *Developing Attachment in Early Years Settings* (David Fulton)

Rook, G. *Regulation of the immune system by biodiversity from the natural environment* (online) (available at www.grahamrook.net)

Sahota, P. Swing into Action (*Nursery World* July 2014)

Szalavitz, M. Perry, B. (2010) *Born for Love* (Harper)

Taylor-Robinson et al. The rise of food poverty in the UK (*BMJ* 2013)

Te Whāriki (available at www.educate.ece.govt.nz)

Tovey, H. All About ...Risk (*Nursery World* January 2014)

Underdown, A. (2006) *Young Children's Health and Wellbeing* (Open University Press)

Whitebread, D. Bingham, S. *School Readiness: a critical review of perspectives and evidence* (TACTYC)

Williams, S. E. Horst, J. S. (2014) *Goodnight Book: sleep consolidation improves word learning via storybooks* (Frontiers in Psychology)

Wolpert, E. (2005) *Start Seeing Diversity: The Basic Guide to an Anti-bias Classroom* (Redleaf Press)

Websites

- www.actionforchildren.org.uk

- www.home-start.org.uk

- www.nspcc.org.uk

- www.parentlineplus.org.uk

- www.adoptionuk.org.uk

- www.afteradoption.org.uk

- www.persona-doll-training.org

- www.rootsofempathy.org

- www.anaphylaxis.org.uk

- www.coeliac.org.uk

- www.pre-school.org.uk (pre-school learning alliance)

- www.naldic.org.uk (supporting children with EAL)

- www.incrediableediblenewtwork.org.uk

- www.ipsea.org.uk (specialised support to parents of special needs children)

- www.jabadao.org.uk (developmental movement play)

- www.inpp.org (institute of neurophysiological psychology)

- www.open-doors-therapy.co.uk (research into motor skills in reception age children)

- www.tommys.org (information for parents-to-be)

- www.bliss.org.uk (premature births)

Apps

- Understanding Child development 0-6 Mobile learning, app free to download from iTunes

Acknowledgements

I have written *Health and Wellbeing* during a time of unforeseen difficulties and personal loss, which made this project even more challenging. I am grateful to the long list of family and friends who have provided me with the physical and emotional support that I needed and helped me to complete the book.

I dedicate it to Elizabeth Anne Counsell (1957-2013).

Many thanks also to:

Vanessa Card and Alice, Matthew, Sam and Olga.

Monica and Neil Jacques, Lottie and P.

Gina Dowding and family.

Tricia Carroll, Tom Webster, Lili and May for their insights into child wellbeing.

Tom and Alex O'Connor.

Mary and Marcel Driver and family.

Julie Fisher, David and Sophie.

Wendy Scott, Cathy Turner and Jasper James Turner.

Natasa Magdalenic and family.

Denise Bailey and Steve Taylor.

Carlene Hutchinson and family.

Emma Aylett, Tony Wilkinson and Frank.

Anna Daly at Primed for Life Training Associates.

Sam Riches and Gwen Atkinson.

Danny O'Connor, for trying his best against all the odds.

Thanks to Angela Shaw at Practical Pre-School Books.

Tajana Ujevic and Anthonia Anagor, and all the staff and children of the nursery and reception class at Kensington Primary, East Ham; Yvette Pullen and Ridge County Primary School, Lancaster; Mary Driver and Trinity St. Michael's Primary School, Croston, Lancashire.